God Wants You Truly Living
Not Walking Dead

*The Journey to God's Abundant Life
Begins With the Death of the
Things That Are Secretly Killing Us*

by
Cinthia Hiett, MC, LPC

Copyright © 2014 by Cinthia Hiett, MC, LPC
All rights reserved. No part of this book may be reproduced, scanned, or distributed in any printed or electronic form without permission.
Revised Edition: November 2014
Printed in the United States of America
ISBN-10: 1502437279
ISBN-13: 978-1502437273

Scripture quotations are taken from the following sources:

The King James Version (KJV).The New King James Version (NKJV®), copyright 1982 by Thomas Nelson, Inc. The Holy Bible, English Standard Version™ (ESV) copyright © 2001 by Crossway Bibles, a division of Good News Publishers. All rights reserved. The Holy Bible, New International Version ® (NIV®). Copyright © 1973, 1978, 1984, International Bible Society.® Used by permission. All rights reserved worldwide. The Message Bible (MSG). Copyright © 1993, 1994, 1995, 1996, 2000, 2001, 2002. Used by permission of NavPress Publishing Group. *Holy Bible,* New Living Translation (NLT), copyright ©1996, 2004, 2007, 2013 by Tyndale House Foundation. Used by permission of Tyndale House Publishers, Inc., Carol Stream, Illinois 60188. All rights reserved. Scripture quotations marked (CEV) are from the Contemporary English Version, Copyright © 1991, 1992, 1995 by American Bible Society, Used by Permission. International Standard Version® and ISV® are Copyright © 1996-forever by The ISV Foundation. ALL RIGHTS RESERVED INTERNATIONALLY. *The Voice Bible* Copyright © 2012 Thomas Nelson, Inc. All rights reserved. Knox Bible. Copyright 2012-2013 © Baronius Press Ltd.

Cover image by Christian Delbert/Shutterstock.com

This book is dedicated to Jesus—
the only One who can give us both
a reason to live and a reason to die.

Table of Contents

Acknowledgments

Introduction...5

Chapter One:
> *A Life Beyond Your Wildest Dreams*................15

Chapter Two:
> *Seeds of Change*..51

Chapter Three:
> *The Death of the Thing That Is Killing Me*..........77

Chapter Four:
> *The Life You're Settling For*..........................127

Chapter Five:
> *How Do I Make the Pain Stop?* 153

Chapter Six:
> *God Is Doing a New Thing*..........................193

Notes..231

Book References, Resources, Recommendations.......233

Sneak Peek: *Can Fairy Tales Be Real?*.......................235

Acknowledgments

It is very difficult to attempt to thank all of the individuals that have made this pursuit possible. Out of all the creative endeavors I have pursued, this was by far the most difficult, the biggest test, and the most arduous task I have ever attempted. I was truly naive as to what it would take, thankfully, or I would have never begun. This was truly a "living and dying" process for me. During the writing of this book, I have handled the dying process in a very personal way as my father faces imminent death in hospice care. I also experienced the loss of my beloved dog, who almost made it to his 18th birthday. I also had to die to independency, to my own timing, to many of my own ideas, and to "my way" (which I really thought was good!). God had a way, He had a message, and He had His time. I came to find it good, blessed, and safe.

I can't thank the Lord enough for including me in the delivery of this message. I continue to be forever, gratefully indebted to Him. I thank God for His wisdom in waiting until I was married to attempt this! Thank you, Michael, my best friend and biggest cheerleader. You always see the best in me and believe in me. I will never forget that one afternoon when you were reading a book and said to me, "Hey, one day you'll be writing one of these pages that thank people for helping you get the book done." Thank you for seeing ahead when I couldn't! Thank you for always encouraging me and for your patience—this was a long journey.

Thank you, Chris. I could have never finished this without you. Your gentle prodding and pushing toward deadlines—and continuing to encourage and believe in this message even when I was so overwhelmed, tired, and just "couldn't get it out" on paper—was invaluable. I would have never finished this if I didn't have you. I would have continued writing forever. Thank you for waiting as I pushed to get things back to you (as you are waiting now for this page).

Thank you for the great editors I had! I do not like writing. It is very difficult for me, and this message would have never become tangible. Thank you Mary and Beth for your patience in this process, for waiting on me, and being so gracious when I continued to add more every time you returned it back to me. I don't know how you do what you do. Thank you for managing and organizing the details so well.

Thank you, mom, for always listening to me, letting me bounce things off of you, and believing that it would get done. Thank you Lisa and Bethany for always laughing and crying with me. And lastly, thank you to all my clients who have enriched my life so deeply and for allowing me to be a part of "your dying process" so that you may have the lives that God has destined for you to have.

Introduction

In the spring of 2011, I was honored to be invited to the largest church in Uganda to speak on the topic of the 11th chapter of John, the story of Lazarus. Alternating between surprise that someone from a continent half a world away was interested in my thoughts and enthusiasm for connecting with another culture, I rose in the pre-dawn hours one morning to phone my contact there to say that yes, I would love to make the trip.

But what I was not anticipating quite so happily? Writing the presentation. If I'm ever fortunate enough to meet you in person, there's one thing you will soon notice about me. Two things, actually: that I have a lot of ideas, and that I'm always happy to tell you about them. I explain, expound, and expand, whether we're out to lunch or I'm presenting at an event. I'm a verbal communicator. Writing a presentation, however, is another matter entirely. It's one of the toughest parts of my job as a psychotherapist. But I know a careful outline and speaking points are essential to good oral communication, so I take my time and do it anyway. It just takes me *a lot* of time.

On that early morning, after making the phone

call, I sat down in my living room, the world outside as dark as the coffee in my mug. I started to jot down a few preliminary thoughts about the presentation. Those thoughts took form, turned into actual notes, which then turned into a presentation—in the space of about forty-five minutes.

Forty-five minutes?!? What happened? Clearly, OD had happened. He gave me a particular message to share with people in Africa first, and now I share them with you in this book. The impetus of the message was John 11 verse 35, which is the shortest verse in the Bible; but it is one of the longest and deepest examples of verses regarding God's concern, compassion, and sympathy for the plight of his people who do not know the outcome as He does. It reads, simply, "Jesus wept."

When I took the message to Africa, I told it to people who didn't have running water, who were dying from AIDS and whose church, as I spoke one night, was being guarded with machine-gun-laden police officers due to the political unrest in the country.

When I shared with them that I earn my living talking to people who are unhappy, depressed, and anxious, they couldn't understand. After all, the Ugandans felt all these things, too—unhappy because of all the political strife that prevented them from feeling safe in their homes; depressed because they, or someone they knew, desperately needed "new blood" due to the AIDS crisis; anxious because they didn't know where their next meal would be coming from, as there was no money to buy food. Quite understandably, they couldn't imagine what Americans would have to be unhappy about.

But Americans, if they were honest with themselves, would be the first people to tell the Ugandans that money—or peace, or even health—can't buy joy. The struggles and pain in Africa are very concrete and very survival-driven. They may suffer from depression, anxiety, and unhappiness, but other needs and shortages are much more pressing. Inner conflict gets ignored; there simply aren't enough resources to address it. The struggles of first-world dwellers, however, are intensely internal. Our physical needs are met, and in our comfort, we become keenly aware that our inner world is a disaster. There are wars inside our minds when we have the time and energy to take a look. We hunger, we thirst—and we're dying. *If we're honest with ourselves.*

While I don't have the answers to end world hunger or spread peace throughout the earth, I can address the inner turbulence we all face through the message that God revealed to me early that morning. Whether you are a distressed Ugandan looking for meaning in the midst of great difficulty, or a comfortable American searching for an ever-elusive happiness, this book can help you put off whatever is weighing you down, so that you can come closer to becoming the best version of yourself—the person your perfect Creator meant you to be. Remember: "for we are not subject to the whims of a sin-stained deity."[1] Instead, He is perfect and all knowing, even when it comes to the trickiest areas of our lives. Although I don't intend for this to be a religious book, the message I have for you has been inspired by God, based on the principles He has established in this world. Wherever you place your trust, or whomever you follow, the way is the same, as are my answers. You don't have to believe in God to benefit from these insights. Just know that what I have to tell you is simply the only successful way I have ever come across to live the abundant life that truly is possible for every human being on this planet, no matter their circumstances.

"Even me?" you may wonder. Perhaps you're facing deep-seated, dark internal pain you've only just begun to sort through. Maybe you're more concerned about physical safety right now. It could be that your life appears to be in working order, but you know it's not. Not really. Or, quite possibly, it seems that your life is just a bundle of messes that no one—not even a higher power—could possibly sort out.

Without tritely saying, "There's always someone who has it worse," I ask you to consider holocaust survivor and Austrian neurologist and psychiatrist Viktor E. Frankl. Like millions of other people, he was exposed to hellish atrocities on a daily basis not much more than 60 years ago. He survived; incredibly, his hope in humanity did, too. He survived by becoming bigger than the trauma; it was not through turning a blind eye, but through clinging to what he knew was good and finding meaning where it looked to others like there was none. My point is not that he, and the others, "had it worse" than we all do, but that he managed to rise above and to discover the abundant life that God had for him, even in a place of death.

This isn't something that we can do on our own. But God wants to help us discover the unique way He will help us get to this point so that we can become our own *best version*, working out the bugs to move closer and closer to what the Designer has in mind for us. You do this for your computer by regularly installing updates so that it operates better than it did a week ago or a year ago. To "update" ourselves in this same way, we must first uncover our bugs and what's holding us captive: the harmful thoughts, actions, behaviors, or relationships that are keeping us from being who we're meant to be.

In fact, we're all dying to something—whether it's denial about a necessary change, selfishness and greed, or a long, dark history of sustained abuse (from others, ourselves, or both)—and none of us will truly live until we've extinguished whatever is ravaging our souls.

I will spend eternity with God and never know, nor fully comprehend, the pain and anguish He has felt over the bondage and abuse of His people, His "kiddos." One of the most moving and meaningful verses to me is Psalm 69:33, which tells us, "The Lord hears the needy and does not despise his captive people" (NIV).

The Message Bible says in the last line of verse 33, "He doesn't walk out on the wretched." He is not mad at us for "living dead" and not knowing how to desire and love life as He knows it. He is not mad at us for being enslaved to things that cause us to "live dead." He is brokenhearted, grieved, and angry at what has happened to His world and His children. God hates death. He just wants to give us back the life that is continuously being stolen from us by our sin, the sins of this world, and by the great oppressor.

What the African people needed, then, is the same thing you and I need: knowledge of God and ourselves rooted in truth. And my message—this book—can lead you to discover the unique way in which God is going to heal and deliver you and me from whatever our unique and personal captivity may be. The result will be that you might live freely and authentically. *What must die for you to truly live?*

Life will still be life. We live on earth, not in heaven. I often say to my clients and myself that if we are believers, this is the closest to hell we will ever get. The only heaven we have on earth is Jesus within us and the ability to experience Him in others. We need heaven on earth. Jesus understood this, and it's why He died. The good news is that it's possible to have God's "kingdom come" when we say "Thy will be done," it just might not look like heaven as we imagine it, or even wish it, to be. Rather, we will see God's kingdom entering our lives through the death of whatever can't exist congruently with His kingdom. In this way, we're privy to a glimpse of heaven. You will

---

In *The Ignatian Way*, imagination is one of the characteristics St. Ignatius used in prayer, as well as in personal reflection. He saw the mind as a storehouse of deep, rich, and fulfilling prayer and felt that a practice of "imaginative prayer" further unlocks that storehouse and creates a deeper, more personal, and more intimate encounter with Jesus.

He taught a method that involved reflecting on a familiar Bible story and placing yourself in the scene, e.g., the feeding of the 5,000.

You join in the crowd to be fed as well. What would you be feeling, what might you see, and what would you hear? What might Jesus be saying or doing, what of the disciples, and the hungry little children?

This is a way to increase our awareness of God in our daily lives and make Jesus' life here on earth more meaningful and relatable.

still face difficulties of all kinds. The difference is that once you've allowed God to overcome the thing that's killing you, and holding you back from the life you're meant to live, you will experience the unbinding of your soul in a way you've never experienced before. It's this God-given freedom that will give you hope, joy, and love in the midst of whatever life may be giving you. In my quest to search out and know God first, then discover God's way of uniquely manifesting His will in my life, I often meditate and pray the following verse:

> This is GOD's Message, the God who made earth, made it livable and lasting, known everywhere as GOD: "Call to me and I will answer you. I'll tell you marvelous and wondrous things that you could never figure out on your own." (Jeremiah 33:2-3 MSG)

God wants to introduce you to someone new: your real self, the one who fits *you* best, fits His plans best and gives you new meaning for your life. It's called "Being Your Own Best Version."[2]

So what's killing you? What are you dying over? We'll begin by discovering what God has in mind when He promises an abundant life and then learn about the two metaphorical types of death we must experience that keep us from this life. One of the ways we will do this is a derivation of *Ignatian Way*: that is, to identify with scriptural characters in a metaphorical way. This enables the Bible to become a more personal experience.

St. Ignatius was more interested in the fruits of the prayer than the method. As a result, we will be looking at several biblical stories and exploring the ways that many of the characters experienced maturity, loss, metaphorical death, and real death. While we don't know exactly the mindsets and situations of each character, we can draw from their experiences to explore human actions and our own spiritual condition. With His truth in mind, we will then look at your own unique captivity and empower you to break free with help from the One who created you. *Let's go find the real you.*

Chapter 1

A Life Beyond Your Wildest Dreams

After his suffering, he showed himself to these men and gave many convincing proofs that *he was **alive**.* (Acts 1:3, NIV, emphasis added)

God can do anything, you know—far more than you could ever imagine or guess, or request even in your wildest dreams! He does it not by pushing us around, but by working within us, his Spirit deeply and gently within us. (Ephesians 3:20 MSG)

The thief comes only in order to steal and kill and destroy. I came that they may have and enjoy life, and *have it in abundance.* (John 10:10 AMP, emphasis added)

What is life? More specifically, what is an *ideal* life? An abundant one? One that fits, and works, and satisfies, even when the world around us is going haywire, as it so often is? What does a life like that even *look* like?

One of the most remarkable things about the most abundant life that was ever lived—by our perfect example, Jesus Christ—is that most of us would say that except for His last few years, it was quite unremarkable. He was a carpenter from a poor town. Nothing about that screams "abundant."

More than that, even the most notable years of Jesus' life, the ones written about, weren't something most people would desire. Jesus had little or no wealth that He held onto and was usually traveling—through highly undesirable places such as Samaria, no less. He was often tired, surrounded by crowds, and expected to speak, and heal, and feed. People whined to Him, belittled Him, battled Him, and turned on Him. At least He had His health—that is, until He was led away to be beaten, crucified, and killed by means of one of the most horrific deaths practiced in all of history.

No, on the outside people wouldn't consider Jesus' life to be particularly abundant. Many of us would say the same about our own. Yet, if Jesus was sent from God, presumably not only to save us from death, but to teach us how to really live, we can assume that He, and God, considered His life to be abundant—ideal, in fact. Isn't that a scary thought?

In this world, Jesus didn't have power, prestige,

popularity, success, good looks, or wealth. Yet, interestingly enough, these are the things that our society counts when they tally up an abundant life. We believe that these things are where happiness lies.

Happiness Lies

How interesting to see these two words side by side: "happiness lies." What an oxymoron. While we all experience happiness throughout our lives, the *pursuit* of happiness leads us astray from better things. Think about holding water in your hands. You must work hard at it, yet it's really only a matter of time before it finds its way out anyway, and, meanwhile, you've wasted your time.

While there's nothing wrong with feeling good, God has much better goals for us than simply being "happy." He realizes that there's no greater joy than being in sync with your purpose.

> *Happiness is a natural outcome of an abundant life.*

On the other hand, the thief (as referred to in John 10:10 at the beginning of this chapter) realizes that if we pursue happiness without seeking out what's truly best for us, we might achieve temporary pleasure. But that only serves to create a bigger void in our lives, so we seek more and more of this brand of counterfeit happiness. The void must be continually fed as it becomes bigger and deeper, screaming loudly to be filled because we know no other happiness, yet we crave what we do not have. King Solomon, a man famed throughout history for his wisdom, put it this way:

> You're addicted to thrills? What an empty life! The pursuit of pleasure is never satisfied. (Proverbs 21:17 MSG)

> I said to myself, "Let's go for it—experiment with pleasure, have a good time!" But there was nothing to it, nothing but smoke. What do I think of the fun-filled life? Insane! Inane! My verdict on the pursuit of happiness? Who needs it? With the help of a bottle of wine and all the wisdom I could muster, I tried my level best to penetrate the absurdity of life. I wanted to get a handle on anything useful we mortals might do during the years we spend on this earth. (Ecclesiastes 2:1-3 MSG)

Countless numbers of people have chased after happiness through traditional means—wealth, power, prestige, etc., only to find it as elusive as an oasis in the desert. What happens, though, if we don't chase after happiness but instead seek the only thing that can leave us fulfilled rather than hungry for more? What if we could actually discover our true purpose? Let's look at the man who did.

The Abundant Life of Jesus

Back to Jesus. He certainly didn't pursue happiness—He was a "man of sorrows." Yet no one could confidently claim that He left this earth unfulfilled, anxious, hopeless, depressed, or angry—many feelings that we battle on a daily basis—even though those were a part of His life. His circumstances were never easy, yet His mind was generally at ease. How could this be? From a psychological standpoint, here's what we know:

- **He was free.** Jesus was free because He understood His power to choose. God can set us free, but we have to choose to live freely and choose not to succumb to captivity. He chose to use His free will to submit to God's will instead of His own self-will. But instead of this tying Him down, it only gave Him more freedom from the constraints the world would have placed upon Him.

- **He had a deep relationship with His Creator.** Enjoying a vertical relationship with God fueled His life, including His relationships with others.

- **He had deep and meaningful relationships with other humans**. People cease to thrive if they are disconnected from other people (think of solitary confinement). There is, however, a responsibility on our part to keep those connections intact. As children (God's children, our parents' children), we're provided with relationships; but as we grow, we need to maintain them. Essentially, if we want to be liked, we must be likable. Jesus was willing to lay down His life for His friends (and even His enemies!), and He died to Himself daily as He related to people on earth, no matter how sad, angry, or tired He felt.
- **He had a clear conscience, never betraying His own value system.** Jesus lived up to His original design; He was true to self. He was a perfect example of what humans were supposed to be like before Adam fell.
- **He realized His value was based solely on being loved by His Father.** Jesus didn't get His identity from how the world felt about

Him, His wealth, good looks, or any of that. Think of a $100 bill. If one were laying in a parking lot, would you pick it up? How about if it were wadded up and covered with mud? What if it had blood on it? The vast majority of us wouldn't hesitate to claim that bill as our own and clean it up. It's the same with people: our value is given to us when we're created. No matter where we've been, or what we have been used for, or how we've been mistreated, or how filthy we've become, no one can change our worth—just as a $100 bill is worth $100, regardless of its journey, use, or condition. It's a $100 bill. Jesus' understanding of this fact fueled His ministry.

- **Lastly, and most importantly, He had meaning and purpose:**

  We are all slaves to whatever masters us (2 Peter 2:19, Romans 6:16). Our most powerful master, slave driver, and captor is our own self-will. In his book, *Man's Search for Meaning,* Viktor Frankl most poignantly describes those prisoners who gave up on life and had lost hope for any future: they were the first to die. Nietzsche says it best:

"He who has a *why* to live for can bear almost any *how*." Jesus was not held captive or hostage to His own self-will. He used His free will as a mortal man to do God's will. Frankl's focus and concern was not why most died, but how anyone could even survive. His Auschwitz experience reinforced one of his key ideas: that life is not the quest for pleasure as Freud believed, or a quest for power, as Adler surmised, but a quest for meaning![3] The way we respond to suffering is what brings profound meaning to our lives. Jesus was able to endure "how" He had to live, because He knew the "why" of His life. Jesus chose life by dying to self. We are prisoners to the wards of life down here. The only way to be free is through God, but we have to choose it.

Jesus fulfilled the very thing He was uniquely created to do without apologizing: to revolutionize peoples' relationship with God or provide an opportunity for a relationship if it wasn't already there. I don't think we can claim that He was happy 100% of the time. But if He regretted His actions, He could have tried to save His own life at any of the opportunities He was given (and there were many!). And He showed none of the anxiety, anger, and all the rest of the emotions that so many of us live with on a daily basis. To pass through life, while accomplishing one's mission, *and* leave it with no regrets? The life of Jesus was an abundant one indeed!

What does this mean to you and me? How can we allow God to infuse in us this abundant life that Jesus walked? Most of us are willing, and probably wanting, to do all the above. However, Jesus took His life one step further in order to enjoy "the abundant life" He professed to offer. What is the one thing Jesus did that had more power, offered more life, and continues to be the defining difference between Him and any other person or entity?

He was willing to lose his life entirely to carry out His purpose. In fact, He knew He would.

Jesus was willing to die for others and to be the final sacrifice that would save them from their sins in obedience to God. But He was also willing to die to Himself. This is evidenced in the great temptation in the desert, where we see that He denied Himself His own comfort by refusing to turn stone into bread, then denying His authority by refusing to jump down from a high place and calling angels to rescue him, and thirdly, resisting the opportunity for accomplishment by refusing to bow down to Satan. It's this dying to self that we'll talk most about in this book.

It's interesting to note that each of these temptations, had He given in, would have killed Him in a sense. It would have killed His purpose and true being in a shorter, easier, faster, and less painful way than His divinely ordained destiny. He understood that in order to be what He was created to be, He had to do it the Creator's way. He had to trust that His Creator knew him to the very core and marrow of His being. Furthermore, He had to trust that His Father, who had created Him, knew the best way, the eternal way, that fulfilled His own uniquely, individually, and authentically designed destiny: the "Jesus Way." It was ultimately the *most abundant* way.

Let us for a moment truly understand the word abundant, or abundance. It means: "being more than enough without being excessive." Think of brimming, bulging, bursting, chock-full, crammed, fat, filled, full, jammed, loaded, packed, saturated, overfilled, overflowing, alive, bursting, and abounding. This is only a glimpse of what God has in mind for us when He uses the word "abundance" to describe the life He came to give us. If your life doesn't feel particularly abundant right now, *something* is holding you back.

God has a rule of always going first and setting

the course; He is "The Way." And what an example He gave us by sacrificing His own Son—God, Himself, incarnate—and dying so that we can have life. If we take this prime act and example one step further, we see that *something* has to die in order to make room for the truly abundant life God is offering His people.

> *There must be a dying process for us to truly live.*

This brings us to the axiom God inspired when I was asked to speak in East Africa on the Story of Lazarus. Now, let us first understand what an axiom is. An axiom is a premise or starting point of reasoning, a universally accepted principle, a self-evident truth that requires no proof. With this understanding, God inspired the following axiom as my message:

"What has to die in order for you to live?"

Did this hit you like a ton of bricks? Dying is permanent; death ends something that once was alive, even thriving. Yet not all things that live in us are meant to be there or to be part of our purpose. I'm thinking of addictions, unhealthy attitudes, and resistance to change; maybe you can think of a few more examples. They're stifling the part of us that *is* meant to live, and thrive, and fulfill God's plans for us—"plans to prosper you, not to harm you, plans to give you hope and a future" (Jeremiah 29:11b, NIV). Prosper…hope…future…no harm: these words ring true for an abundant life, even if the world around us is less than ideal. But first comes the dying part. **There must be a dying process for us to truly live**, and it's not something we can do on our own.

However, our great God has gone before us and knows the way. He does not grow tired and understands that suffering through death produces life. He also promises us comfort through suffering and tells us in Psalm 138:8 that "the Lord will fulfill his purpose for me" (ESV).

> All praise to the God and Father of our Master, Jesus the Messiah! Father of all mercy! God of all healing counsel! He comes alongside us when we go through hard times, and before you know it, He brings us alongside someone else who is going through hard times so that we can be there for that person just as God was there for us. We have plenty of hard times that come from following the Messiah, but no more so than the good times of His healing comfort—we get a full measure of that, too. (2 Corinthians 1:3-5 MSG)

And now, we need to look at Jesus in a new light. He lived an abundant life—and also one that's meant to be an example...not just of how to love and treat others, but also how to die to oneself to gain life. Jesus is the consummate "servant leader"; He leads the way by example. He doesn't just teach a concept, He walks it out fully and completely before asking or expecting us to walk the same path. Yet again, He promises us in Psalms 23:4: "Even though I walk through the Valley of the Shadow of Death I will fear no evil, for you are with me, your rod and staff, they comfort me." Please note that shadows cannot happen without light. God shines while we are in dark places so that we may see the "why" and the "how" as well as the "WAY."

I'll put it to you again: "What has to die in order for you to live?" There are two types of death that need to happen in order to produce and/or sustain life:

1. The death of a good thing in order to become the best thing. The "best thing" is usually what the person is destined or created for.
2. The death of the thing that is killing me.

Realize that if the first thing isn't allowed or encouraged to die, it will *most likely* kill the real me. Like a parasite. The second, however, will most assuredly kill me—more quickly, like a predator. If you look closely, you'll notice that you can see examples of both at various times in your life. Your challenge? To allow God to guide you through your own unique dying process so that you can come into the abundant life God died for you to live!

Just as Jesus did, you'll need to use your free will to surrender your self-will to God's will. Remember that in the Old Testament, when people didn't have the power and freedom of the Holy Spirit, God resorted to death to accomplish His will. In fact, we can learn a lot from the ancient traditions, many of which, interestingly enough, haven't been commonly practiced since shortly after Jesus left the earth. Animal sacrifices were given hourly, daily, monthly, yearly—all the time in the Old Testament to atone for the Jewish people's sins. Jesus came, however, as the ultimate sacrifice for the sins of this world: a sacrifice that is complete and never needs to be repeated.

> **Just as Jesus did, you'll need to use your free will to surrender your self-will to God's will.**

The Jewish temple was destroyed in 70 CE, and the Jewish people are still waiting for the Messiah to establish a temple in which they may worship and offer sacrifices to God. Christians, however, realize that just as these animal sacrifices are no longer necessary, *we* are the temple. Christ lives in us. We, then, can offer sacrifices of ourselves in our dying process—our will, our wishes, our desires, our own way, and anything else that needs to die so the Lord can free us from sin and complete the good work within us. We must sacrifice daily to the Lord so that we may truly live.

The choice given to people in the Old Testament was to serve God, men, self, or Satan. In the New Testament and beyond, we choose to serve our self-will, Satan's will, or God's will. He wants willing servants as He accomplishes His will.

This will be Uncomfortable.

There's nothing about the dying process, and the change that inherently comes with it, that feels natural. It's new; we've never done it before. To permanently rid your life of a habit, a thought process, a way of living, or your life's dream, takes immense courage. Not to mention the new habits or thought processes required to replace the ones that haven't been helpful. Death here means putting an end to anything that's holding you back and dying to your own will as a way to make room for God's will. During or after this type of dying process, you might be required to come to terms with significant life changes you've been running from, to develop or relinquish a key relationship, to change how you view the world, to begin new customs or abolish old ones. No, this will not be comfortable—but it will be worth it.

The difficulty in this process is that there is not a formula for achieving the abundant life. In this book, I can explain what is happening and give you much knowledge that may even lead to understanding; however, this does not automatically lead to wisdom and change. Instead, the only way out is *through*. Each of us has a unique growth and developmental process that must be embraced, explored, and walked out. This is the journey to becoming your own best version in any and every season of your life. It has never been done before.

> **Each of us has a unique growth and developmental process that must be embraced, explored, and walked out.**

So, the bad news is that there's no bright and shiny "3-Step Plan for Your Dying Process and Subsequent Abundant Life." Personally, this makes me uncomfortable. I like to feel in control of a process and to understand what's happening—especially if it's happening *to* me. That's how I feel peace, even in uncertainty. I feel like I can handle anything if I can understand it, if I can make sense of it. But peace without understanding means *trust*. Ouch!! Trusting is a lot less comfortable than understanding! Be that as it may, I find that the Lord continuously desires to give us peace that *passes* all understanding. In other words, peace that is beyond anything I can comprehend; so striving for complete understanding of the Lord's work in me will do me no good. This tells me that I must stop *needing* to understand absolutely everything in my life, but rather accept that God has a way. Furthermore, I must accept that I will probably not comprehend His way, nor will I be able to understand His way before it occurs. If I don't accept God's way, I am relegated to my way, which, as I have continuously proved, does not work!

Even if the dying process—the process of letting go of whatever is killing the real me—feels strange and unfamiliar, and raises more questions than answers at first, there will be peace in it. The other good news is that you don't need to go through this alone. Just as Jesus relied fully on His relationship with His God and Father, you can too. Jesus spent long nights praying; He sought refuge by praying and opening His heart to God in solitary places. You can too, and God will not disappoint. This is why I love when the psalmist says in 138:8: "The Lord will fulfill his purpose for me; your love, O Lord, endures forever—do not abandon the works of your hands" (NIV). In The Message Bible version, the last phrase reads, simply, "Don't quit on me now!" God might also say the same to us: "People, don't quit on me now; I am not finished with the good work I have begun in you."

Believe me, I know it can be very frustrating to not see the whole picture, to not know everything that's going on. Consider that one of the reasons for this is that God wants a relationship with us more than anything. He wants to be a part of His unique plan and process that's going to work in you and me. He wants to be part of the one He has made, and the one He wants to dwell with eternally.

What's more, He wants us to begin to know Him on a deeper level. His plan is a journey of discovery, and it can only be uncovered and integrated through knowing something of our Creator. In fact, when He reveals Himself to you, you are revealed to yourself at the same time; in the process of knowing our Creator, we begin to know ourselves. As I like to put it, the more I see God in me, the more I see the "real" me: the person God had in mind when He created me. And as we know ourselves better, we begin to see things that are contrary to His creation. I see those things that are killing His creation, my true self, and stealing from the life of abundance God has destined for me. These are things we can't know until we have a deeper understanding of God Himself, and this deeper understanding can't be gained in a day or through a typical 3-step process.

We need to accept that we cannot comprehend the process; just as a caterpillar has no comprehension of the butterfly but willingly allows for the process of transformation. We need to trust what God has planted in us, the seed of our identity that must be fulfilled. He will complete the good work He has begun in us—if we are willing. We need to trust the One who died for us, otherwise known as Jesus, and "His Way." We get a beautiful word picture of this in the 14th chapter of John (NIV):

> ***Then he said to his disciples, "Why can't you trust me?"***

> Thomas said to him, "Lord, we don't know where you are going, so how can we know the way?" Jesus answered, "I am the way and the truth and the life. No one comes to the Father except through me. If you really know me, you will know my Father as well. From now on, you

do know him and have seen him." (John 14:5-7)

We all like to understand what is happening to us, but this doesn't always mean that we understand the ways of God. It's like explaining a mortgage to a seven-year-old. Even if he could comprehend it, he still has to depend on his parents to provide for him. He does his part, just as we do our part; but ultimately, he will continue to spend his allowance on toys and candy rather than contributing to a current or future mortgage.

> ***And the peace of God, which transcends all understanding, will guard your hearts and your minds in Christ Jesus.***
> ***Philippians 4:7 (NIV)***

Just the same, we don't understand all of God's big plans for our lives. Understanding and maturity may lead to better decisions, but we will never attain the same level of wisdom as our Creator. God is telling us that His ways are not our ways; His thoughts are not our thoughts; yet He still has our best interest in mind.

> Look at the birds of the air; they do not sow or reap or store away in barns, and yet your heavenly Father feeds them. Are you not much more valuable than they? (Matthew 6:26 NIV)

God could attempt to explain, just as we might patiently open our financial records for our seven-year-old to see. Knowledge, however, can be present without understanding, and understanding does not always lead to wisdom.

We still need God's wisdom to guide us through life; and in seeking God's way, we also have to accept His process. Without God, I would seek peace through understanding.

But, many times, His way is peace without understanding. This is the definition of trust, and trust is what we need in undertaking our journey.

> Then he said to his disciples, "Why can't you trust me?" They were in absolute awe, staggered and stammering, "Who is this, anyway? He calls out to the winds and sea, and they do what he tells them!" (Luke 8:25 MSG)

Why can't we trust him? I need to remind myself in whom I am trusting and whose ways I believe in. Not my ways, not my thoughts, but the one who calms the storms with a word, the one who raises the dead, the one who conquers death, and the one who died for me.

His Ways are Not Our Ways.

"I want to know all God's thoughts, the rest are just details." (Albert Einstein 1879-1955)

> "For my thoughts are not your thoughts, neither are your ways my ways, declares the Lord. As the heavens are higher than the earth, so are my ways higher than your ways and my thoughts than your thoughts." (Isaiah 55:8-9 NIV)

> "I don't think the way you think. The way you work isn't the way I work." GOD's Decree. "For as the sky soars high above earth, so the way I work surpasses the way you work, and the way I think is beyond the way you think. Just as rain and snow descend from the skies and don't go back until they've watered the earth, doing their work of making things grow and blossom, producing seed for farmers and food for the hungry, so will the words that come out of my mouth not come back empty-handed. They'll do the work I sent them to do, they'll complete the assignment I gave them. (Isaiah 55:8-11 MSG)

There's one thing you can count on when it comes to God's change process in you. It will be like nothing you've experienced before. It probably won't make much sense at times. But that, in and of itself, makes sense. After all, if you let Him, God will rid you of the parts of your past and your personal day-to-day things that are strangling you—things that seem normal now. Parts of you must die so that others can live. It's a big deal.

Consider a map. We trust that the person who drew it has been there before—not only to the destination, but the whole route and vicinity the map covers. We haven't visited the place, but we have confidence that the mapmaker can lead us correctly. A map has limits, however. There are many things that can't be seen, experienced, or anticipated with a map. We rely on the map, but we also need the accompanying wisdom. If God's word is the map, then the life of Jesus, His parables and His teachings are the guidebook. Jesus's wisdom transcends time, culture, and education (remember He was also a prophet); they can guide us today as we undertake the journey to unleash our abundant life.

Again, we see the life of Jesus as our example. Just how did he take God's map for Him, and use it to live out His real, true, and best self? He, himself, died. For us, that means that on this journey to becoming God's ultimate version of ourselves, we need to consider the second type of death necessary in having a truly abundant life. We need to allow God to abolish whatever is killing us—to transform our lives as we know them.

> Whoever tries to keep their life will lose it, and whoever loses their life will preserve it. If you cling to your life, you will lose it, and if you let your life go, you will save it. (Luke 17:33 NIV, NLT)

Living the "crucified life" is vastly different from being the living dead. When Jesus rose, He gave many convincing proofs that He was, indeed, alive. He then returned, alive, to heaven. Life is the central theme; death was only a means to an end. By being willing to die to what's killing our abundant life, through God's own processes, we will find life on a different level—a new life that turns our past life into a mere shadow.

> **Living the "crucified life" is vastly different from being the living dead.**

Perhaps you're thinking that you don't particularly want to journey to death—even with a map and a guidebook! You're not alone. But consider the words of Albert Einstein: "God always takes the simplest way." Take heart that God hates unnecessary pain; He's not a sadist! He won't take us through any trial He doesn't have to. No matter how difficult the path, it is truly the easiest and safest route. In fact, any path He doesn't lead us on will undoubtedly lead to hazardous places. Consider the 23rd Psalm (NIV) as a description of the path God has prepared for you:

> The Lord is my shepherd, I lack nothing. He makes me lie down in green pastures, he leads me beside quiet waters, he refreshes my soul. He guides me along the right paths for his name's sake. Even though I walk through the darkest valley I will fear no evil, for you are with me; your rod and your staff, they comfort me. You prepare a table before me in the presence of my enemies. You anoint my head with oil; my cup overflows. Surely your goodness and love will follow me all the days of my life, and I will dwell in the house of the Lord forever.

> Forget the former things; do not dwell on the past. See, I am doing a new thing! Now it springs up; do you not perceive it? I am making a way in the wilderness and streams in the wasteland. (Isaiah 43:18-19 NIV)

Therefore, if anyone is in Christ, the new creation has come: The old has gone, the new is here! (2 Corinthians 5:17 NIV)

Yes, you must die in order to truly live. But when you die through God's processes, you are given a new, abundant future. God was doing, and did, a new work in the life of the *human* Jesus. He certainly can, and will, do the same in you!

Reflection questions:
Each chapter in this book will include a reflection section in the form of a workbook. Speaking honestly, I am one of the worst offenders of not completing workbook sections. I like to read and reflect; but I avoid the tough work of application if at all possible (remember I don't like to write). This is not a good thing! It's not enough to hope what we read is absorbed—we need to ensure that it is; writing and applying help us to truly "get it."

You're welcome to ignore these workbook sections and go back to them after you've read the book in its entirety or to complete them as you go. Please do not feel overwhelmed by the amount of questions, nor compelled to answer all of them, as the list can be fairly exhaustive. The questions are plentiful; pick the ones that fit you and may inspire new ones of your own. Use the reflection questions you feel are being prompted by God. Ask the Lord for wisdom, guidance, and direction as to what questions to answer, when to answer, and how much is needed, as well as what questions the Holy Spirit may be prompting that I may not have included. This is truly *your* book, your process; ask God for insight and enlightenment. However, if you skip them completely, you most likely will not benefit to the degree you desire.

In addition, I highly recommend that you journal your thoughts, feelings, and responses to what you are reading. I'm probably less fond of journaling than you are, but I do it because it really helps me process the information. I also mark up sections, bend corners and truly "live in" the book I am reading; this way I can make my own journey and map. By doing this we are allowing the process to move from just "head knowledge" to actual "heart change" and healing.

With that in mind, please consider and complete the following questions.

1. When did a transition alter your life, and what changes did you have to make?

2. Which one of the following principles from this chapter seem the most difficult for you to

understand or put into practice? For example: Which type of death resonates within my heart and mind? What is God revealing to me, or telling me, when I read the verse in Isaiah which says: "God's ways are not our ways." What might God be saying to me about Isaiah 43:18-19? What "new thing" do I need to perceive? These are few of the concepts in the chapter that you may want to consider and meditate on. Ask the Lord what resources you have, or need, that you could use when addressing these concepts?

3. How have your culture, family, and your experience contributed to the difficulty regarding these concepts?

4. On a scale of 1 to 10, with 10 being the highest, where would you rate:
   a. Your resistance to God's will
   b. Your fear of God's will
   c. Your faith in God's will
   d. Your understanding of God's will
   e. Your desire for God's will
   f. Your willingness to die to self-will and use your free will to embrace God's will?

5. What resources or help do you need in order to allow God to actively work in your life?
    a. Mentoring, discipling, counseling, accountability, or other types of support.
    b. Asking God for willingness to help with your resistance (or, in other words, *the want to "want to"*).
    c. Consider reading Scripture regularly, five minutes a day to start, or just reading Proverbs. Open your ears to hear God's word by reading and listening and making time for a relationship with God. Consider reading Scripture by using the "Ignatian Way."

6. On a scale of 1 to 10 (10 being very resistant, 1 being very open), how resistant are you to surrendering to God's will in your life? What *can* you do to move yourself one notch closer to surrendering?

7. Ask God to show you a particular area of your life that you need to surrender to Him. Then, ask Him to show you one way you can do this. Be watching for His responses in the next few days and weeks.

8. Ask the Lord to tell you what changes you have made and what you're doing right. It is very important to ask the Lord this question. He wants to encourage us, and He is not as critical of us as we are of ourselves.

9. Meditate on the John 10:10 Scripture verse, maybe even look it up in several translations. When you consider that the *thief comes to kill, steal, and destroy* (John 10:10), what, when, and how do you see this manifested in your life? Ask the Lord for wisdom, knowledge, grace, and energy to resist the "wrong" things being killed. Also, ask for insight into how God is using Romans 8:28 *(That's why we can be so sure that every detail in our lives of love for God is worked into something good. MSG)* as a way to encourage us, and strengthen us, as we experience the dying process in our lives here on earth.

10. How do you feel, and what do you think, about God using death to bring abundance in your life?

11. What did your parents, or significant other adults, believe was the "abundant life" for you? Be honest with yourself; only you and God need to see these answers.

12. As a child under the age of twelve, what did you believe an abundant life looked like? Was it being president, exploring outer space as an astronaut, or creating your own version of Willy Wonka's Chocolate factory? Maybe becoming a princess or a professional baseball player? What were your dreams as an adolescent? What got you through your teenage years? God's will may be a version of those dreams you had. He gave me a great insight into dreams and fairy tales through the following analogy: I live in Phoenix, Arizona, and there is a great mountain called "South Mountain." At one time in my life, God pointed me in the direction of this mountain. However, I soon learned He didn't want me to *go* to this mountain; He wanted me to go *in the direction* of this mountain. My real destination was Mexico City, and South Mountain is on the way. This showed me that God oftentimes inspires dreams that can help move me in the direction of a bigger dream that I *cannot* see. We'll use this type of insight in later chapters as we look at using our "free will" to give up "self-will" and choose "God's will." It is imperative to understand the "childlike" part of ourselves that may have been disillusioned by God and/or

life. Maybe we once had a dream and, even though we may now know it is childish, it was filled with hope! This step of reconciling the adult abundant life with the childhood dreams that were so very intense, powerful, and poignant is imperative to healing and receiving the abundant life. You see, God takes these dreams very seriously and does not make light of them, nor does He scoff at them. Who knows how close our childhood dreams might have been if we were not relegated to a fallen world!

13. As a teenager, what were your dreams? Realize the use of the term "abundant life" is quite an adult term. As a result, accessing earlier childhood/teenage hopes might be better found when using terms such as dreams, hopes, and visions.

14. As a young adult, how did these dreams, visions, hopes, or desires change, if at all? If they have died, how painful has that been for you?

15. Are you dealing with the death of a dream? Is a dream currently dying? What is the dream you have to let go of? How has it affected your relationship with God? Do you need to forgive

God? (This does not mean that God did anything wrong; it simply means we got hurt. Many times people may hurt our feelings without doing anything wrong, but we still need to forgive them. This is a necessary part of relationship. We must forgive when we are let down, disappointed, feel mislead, or feel that our desires and wishes are not taken seriously. Maybe you feel you are the reason the dream was unfulfilled, that you messed up, or that you missed something? These are important things to reconcile with God in order to have the freedom necessary to experience the abundance God has for you.)

16. How about *now?* At the age you are living, what ideas of the abundant life have persisted?

17. Which ones have remained constant? Remember there are no wrong answers—just your honest, authentic, and thoughtful insights.

18. What does God say? Work to avoid legalism with your answer; this is not from God.

19. Are there any aspects of your present life that you feel are part of the abundant life God has given you now? Take some time and meditate

on the following verses, using the questions at the end to prompt you in hearing "God's Way" for you:

Discipline in a Long-Distance Race
Do you see what this means—all these pioneers who blazed the way, all these veterans cheering us on? It means we'd better get on with it. Strip down, start running—and never quit! No extra spiritual fat, no parasitic sins. Keep your eyes on Jesus, who both began and finished this race we're in. Study how he did it. Because he never lost sight of where he was headed—that exhilarating finish in and with God—he could put up with anything along the way: cross, shame, whatever. And now he's there, in the place of honor, right alongside God. When you find yourselves flagging in your faith, go over that story again, item by item, that long litany of hostility he plowed through. That will shoot adrenaline into your souls! (Hebrews 12:2 MSG)

1. *How do you need to "get on with it"?*
2. *Have you lost sight of where you're headed, or have you never received "sight" about where you are headed?*

3. *Can you/will you "put up with anything" along the way? Even "putting up with" yourself?*
4. *Are you struggling with your faith? Go over God's story again for you.*

Chapter 2

SEEDS OF CHANGE: THE DEATH OF A GOOD THING TO BECOME THE BEST THING

Any transition serious enough to alter your definition of self will require not just small adjustments in your way of living and thinking but a full-on metamorphosis.
Marcus Aurelius Antoninus, 121 AD - 180 AD, *Meditations*

The only constant is change.
Herakleitos of Ephesus, 535-475 BC

The death of the past allows for a true experience of the present and its infinite quest of the future.
Cinthia Hiett, April 2013

We've all heard it before: the only constant is change. And one thing that's clear in the Bible is that God allows change, plans change, and He is always using change in our lives. Big changes, little changes, life-changing changes. That's because, whether we like it or not, He wants to change our lives and to mold us into better versions of ourselves—the people He knows we can become. Always, forever, for better. And there's never an end to the work that needs to be done.

What has changed in your life? Have you had an addition to your family by way of a new baby, a new spouse, stepchildren, or a pet? Have you experienced the unexpected or expected loss of a baby, a spouse (to divorce or death), a pet, a brother or sister, a friend, a parent, or a co-worker? How about a job change by your choice, or maybe it was thrust upon you? Maybe an unexpected demotion or promotion? Or in today's world, just added responsibility? What about a move, a bigger house, or the loss of a house? What if you experienced fire or a break-in? How about a major physical change—perhaps you became pregnant, gained weight, or lost weight, or are losing your hair? Were you injured or did you have something corrected? How about a prolonged illness that you did not expect? Did you win the lottery, did someone steal your life's savings, or did you go through a bad business deal or investment? What if you just noticed, or are having to face the fact, that you really are aging? Or remember when you entered puberty? These are all examples of change that create stress and loss—even the good changes.

God works for the good of those He loves. But

just as a parent might require a child who hates the water to take swim lessons, for their own good, God might allow job loss, a cross-country move, a pregnancy, and myriad other circumstances to shape the lives of His children. Sometimes these are happy changes we've been hoping and praying for; sometimes, they leave us reeling in their wake.

Either way, *all* changes, even positive ones, produce stress and create loss. Winning the lottery can be stressful, even though we might gain some degree of financial security. What we thought would simplify things (not needing to worry about money) might complicate our lives more than ever. Friends and family might think of us differently, not to mention the fact that we might be quitting jobs and moving to warmer locations. All life changes cause us to make adjustments in our lives, thereby challenging our comfort level.

> *"We can have pain for gain, or pain in vain, but we can never have no pain."*

As you'd expect, humans usually dislike and resist stress and loss, the byproducts of change. We know for a fact that change is *at the least* uncomfortable and, at most, excruciatingly painful. We choose pleasure and comfort instead, and who wouldn't? Therefore, stress always creates a critical juncture for us: Are we going to let the pain created by this change be in vain, or will we allow the pain of change to be for gain because we know there is never "no pain"? In other words, "We can have pain for gain, or pain in vain, but we can never have *no pain*."

There is never "no pain." In fact, not only did God design people to handle stress, He designed them to benefit from it. Stress creates change, and change creates stress, but the result of this pattern is seen in new strength, beauty, and depth. This only happens if we allow it, because we can decide how we respond to stress, change, and the pain it brings. Many people choose to dig their heels into the ground and resist change with everything they've got. This type of attitude results in the development of defense mechanisms such as avoidance, resistance, control, aggression, numbing, disassociation, intellectualization, or manipulation, to name a few. These reactions were created by us, *not God*, to protect us and our status quo. Although they may help us *survive* our life (with its stressors and changes), they do not help us to *thrive*. Instead, they leave us wandering in a maze of misery as

> *"If there is anything good in a person, pain will find it out."*

we try to deny the exact changes that God wants to use for our good.

I assume you're reading this book because you want to thrive. My message to you in this chapter is that it's vital for you to *accept* the changes God has allowed and planned in your life, every one of them, and through His power and guidance, let Him use them to bring about a more abundant life for you. There will be pain, but you will be amazed at the work God can do!

There is a plethora of literature that expresses the resultant beauty of pain. We have example upon example, story upon story, that exemplifies this phenomenon. You see, "If there is anything good in a person, pain will find it out." This works in the inverse as well as we study the story of Job. Look at how he responded, versus how his wife responded, to the horrible changes and loss they had to face and endure. And yet, it must bring God such heartache to see that, more often than not, pain brings out the best in humans. Unfortunately, ease and pleasure produce nothing valiant or admirable on their own; they are intended to be a reward or outcome as a byproduct of overcoming or enduring some great and painful hardship. And these do come, eventually, after the change and the stress. Like we see every winter and spring, the old has to die for the new to come. There are seasons for a reason.

We see this time and time again in nature. Consider the parable of the seed.

> I tell you the truth, unless a kernel of wheat falls to the ground and dies, it remains a single seed. But if it dies, it produces many seeds. (John 12:24 NIV)

Anyone can count the seeds in an apple, but only God can count the apples in a seed. (Robert H. Schuller)

Every loss has a gain, and every gain has a loss.

Let's think for a minute about seeds. A seed is nothing special in and of itself. We don't revere seeds, we don't admire them, and we are not in awe of seeds. On the contrary, we look forward only, anxiously, to the "bloom," or the seed's fruition.

A seed must die in order to live the life for which it is intended. We are the seeds God has placed on this earth, and we are the people God intends to bring to fruition. What's the seed in you that must die in order for God to cause it to bloom?

Seeds are intended to be something; there's an intent behind each seed, whether it's the beginnings of an oak tree or a single blade of grass. There's an intent in us, too, of an original creation waiting to come out. What we shouldn't do is protect the seed, nurture it into staying exactly as it is, or even ease its growth unnecessarily. Nor should we abandon the seed or starve it. It might be buried deeply, waiting out its natural cycle before it germinates, but it still needs water and nourishment. Instead, let it burst forth!

> *"I must to be willing to give up what I am, in order to become what I will be."*
> *- Albert Einstein*

The important thing to remember, though, is that the seed must die, or change, before it can live; it must break out of the outward shell that is holding it captive. Compare the metaphors of a caterpillar turning into a butterfly and a tadpole becoming a frog. If the necessary metamorphoses are prematurely interrupted or unnaturally delayed, the organism itself will not survive. We are used to bondage, and sameness, but that doesn't mean that it is a *good* thing.

We see this happening in the movie, *Failure to Launch*. The production may have its humorous moments, but the reality of this story is tragic—a full-grown adult still lives with and relies on his parents, and likes it that way, as do they. But this phenomenon isn't limited to the big screen, as we see it played out in our culture, our families, and our marriages. What a tragedy for the individual who never becomes all he or she was destined to be—just like an acorn that thinks it's only an acorn, a caterpillar that thinks it's only a caterpillar, or a tadpole that intends to be a tadpole forever.

> *"He cuts off every branch of mine that doesn't produce fruit, and he prunes the branches that do bear fruit so they will produce even more."*
> *John 15:2 NLT*

A similar tragedy is seen in the story of the first humans created. Adam and Eve were exposed to knowledge before their maturity would support it—they "launched" too soon. Their resultant, poorly chosen action of opposing their Creator destroyed the creative process He had for their lives. When we go against creation, and interrupt or impede God's timing, the creation either dies or fails to thrive. The same tragedy occurs when a butterfly is prematurely taken out of its cocoon. The enzymes necessary to create the wings only happen in the struggle to get out of the cocoon that was most recently protecting it. Further travesties occur when children are either not encouraged to grow up, want to grow up too soon in order to "do it their way," or need to grow up sooner than they should. "He cuts off every branch of mine that doesn't produce fruit, and he prunes the branches that do bear fruit so they will produce even more" (John 15:2 NLT).

We know, then, that God has a plan for us *when* He has a plan for us and *how* He has a plan for us. It's the "how" and sometimes the "when" that can trip us up. It just seems that sometimes the trials and sufferings are so darn inconvenient! But consider the alternative—zero growth, zero potential, zero abundance. It's not that God can't work with any life situation; it's that He's choosing to work with yours, where you're at, by moving you to another place, whether spiritually, emotionally, intellectually, or physically. Yes, He does want to change you, because He knows how wondrous His plans are for you.

> "My dear child, are you wondering at the sequence of trials in your life? Behold that vineyard and learn of it. The gardener ceases to prune, to trim, to harrow, or to pluck the ripe fruit only when he expects nothing more from the vine during that season. It is left to itself, because the season of fruit is past and further effort for the present would yield no profit.

Comparative uselessness is the condition of freedom from suffering. Do you then wish me to cease pruning your life? Shall I leave you alone?" And the comforted heart cried, "No!"[4]

God knows there is pain involved in growth. If we resist God's pruning or training, we are resisting the good, or helpful, pain; but that's no protection against the pain the rest of life offers. As I mentioned before, you can have pain for gain, or pain in vain, but there is never no pain. Resisting God's work in our lives means the pain experienced will be in vain. God will allow us to suffer the pain that comes from resisting Him and banning Him from our lives, but the pain will only be in vain as it produces only frailty, fragility, cynicism, jadedness, bitterness, stronger defense mechanisms, and more self-medicating behaviors, such as addictions. Do you know people like this?

You see, God will leave us alone to face these if we decide not to allow Him to be involved. This occurs when we use our free will to do our own self-will. One thing's for sure: whether we choose "pain in vain" or "pain for gain" we ensure that we will increase pain. However, the good that the Lord provides regarding the inevitability of pain is outcome. By choosing the type of pain (i.e. pain for gain or pain in vain), we invariably choose life or death.

Remember His promises: to prosper you, not to harm you, and to lead you beside still waters. "I will cause the shower to come down in his season; there shall be showers of blessing" (Ezekiel 34:26 KJV). There are seasons of mourning and drought, just as there are seasons of richness and blessing; and each one is part of the abundant life.

Change, Change, Change

Let's take a closer look at change. Changes come in three types. And each type treats you differently. Here they are:

1. A change you initiate: this may include an intentional job change, a marriage (or possibly divorce), an addition to the family, a move, a pursuit of higher education.
2. A change that's predictable, but unavoidable: aging (including puberty), a progression through a job or education, new neighbors.
3. A change that's unforeseen and out of our hands: an illness, a natural disaster, job loss, winning the lottery.

Another type of change worth mentioning is the loss of a dream or vision. This is not a small thing; it can be just as big as the loss of a loved one, and quite often more complicated. It is a pervasive and overarching loss that can lead us to lose faith if we don't handle it appropriately.

The loss of a dream must be dealt with appropriately and very seriously or one can lose their faith. Maybe you know that feeling. It might sound like, "It doesn't matter anymore. I still believe in God, but what's the point?" Maybe the loss of a person, or a job, or your social standing, or the hope of a family, or what you perceive your calling to be, has left you despondent and despairing. It is a nebulous, vague, loss that is difficult to describe to people, and it is often not taken as seriously as it should be. But this type of loss is like a cancer in our souls if left unattended or unaddressed. We scream, "Why? Why God? This makes no sense to me; how does this help You and Your kingdom?" These are the cries of many of God's best; you're not alone. We heard this throughout the book of Job, when he cried to God saying, "It would have been better if I were never born" (Job 3:1). Or when King David says, "What good am I to you in the grave?" (Psalm 30:9) and wonders about the point of his suffering.

What is the point? The loss of the dream is one of the greatest trials of our faith because it is so deeply personal. It is very frightening and disorienting to us when we are not sure who God is anymore—and understandably so! But so often, our trials, our disappointments, our hopes, our ways, our thoughts, and our dreams imprison us and stifle us from becoming who we're meant to be. They limit us in that we only see *our* solution, *our* way out, or *our* way for a meaningful life.

> **We have lost our vision, not realizing that "our way" may need to die in order for us to see the greater vision God has for us.**

Unfortunately, many of us are willing to die there, being the walking dead versus living a crucified life. We have lost our vision, not realizing that "our way" may need to die in order for us to see the greater vision God has for us. We need to trust that God has a greater good that will result from this great loss (Romans 8:28) if we allow for the grief and loss process, even if we don't know when the greater good may appear. In truth, sometimes we need these things removed, and we need to be sequestered by God to allow the maturing process to take place so that we can grow and develop uninterrupted in understanding the workings of the Holy Spirit. We will then eventually take our places as the spiritually mature people God has intended us to be.

Closely tied to this is the death of a good thing,

and possibly a thing that *shouldn't* have died. Be that as it may, it has died for one reason or another. God can still do an even better thing in our lives. We'll see this a bit later with Job's story: he had no clue whether he would even survive his ordeal, let alone that it could be used to bring him more good in his life than he'd ever had before.

Each change we face in our lives can be described as positive or negative, predictable or not, and avoidable or not; but still it's a death—something dies with every change. What's more, every loss has a gain, and every gain has a loss. But that's only the beginning. It's a little-known fact that most lottery winners end up more miserable than when they started. Whereas people who experience great loss can, and do, find great joy in life again. How does that work?

Typically, it's in how people *respond* to the change that makes it; after all is said and done, it's either a positive or negative experience. A negative response to change might mean a lack of coping skills, an inability to manage the stress well, a tendency to rely on defense mechanisms, resistance to the grief and loss process, and a general fear of pain itself. This can be the case whether the change is considered positive or negative at the outset (for example, graduating from college and needing to find a job, versus losing a job and being in the same position of needing to find a new one). If these are present in our response to change, the outcome will most likely be negative, even if the change is positive.

If, however, we effectively manage the loss or gain, with the stress that is incurred and is mandatory for success and growth to happen, we can expect to *grow*—to gain a part of the abundance God wants and plans for us. This type of growth produces depth, character, wisdom, substance, and maturity. These qualities are indicative of a "safe" person, a trustworthy person, a godly person. Changes and losses will occur, but part of managing and growing is the willingness to accept them as they are. We can't prevent suffering, but we can ease the pain for others and ourselves by allowing God to help us.

Let's take a closer look at a negative reaction to change, grief, and loss. When people find themselves unable to manage these effectively, defense mechanisms become the coping strategy. A defense mechanism is an automatic or unconscious drive to protect oneself from the threat of emotional pain. This, in and of itself, is not bad. Healthy defense mechanisms are given to us by God as a way to grow and mature and become all He has made us to be. For example, a healthy physical defense mechanism may be seen in our reflex reactions: our bodies can think "for" us and even save our lives or someone else's. We will look at healthy psychological defense mechanisms, which are typically referred to as "healthy coping skills" in a later chapter.

Negative or unhealthy defense mechanisms are very problematic, not only for ourselves but also for those around us. They generally develop as an attempt to protect the ego. These ego defense mechanisms are generally employed to *defend* our self-images from the pain of shame, guilt, rejection, etc. as well as to attempt to maintain position, power, or the ability to get what the person thinks they need. Some of the most common defense mechanisms are Avoidance, Control, Resistance, Aggression, Manipulation, Disassociation, Intellectualizing, Displacement, Rationalization, Withdrawal, Isolating, and Numbing.

In truth, we all fall into using negative ego defense mechanisms to varying degrees, simply due to the imperfect world we were born into and the sin nature we inherited. The higher the degree, intensity, and prevalence, the more the dysfunction, character issues, and sin we will see manifested within our lives. The practice of negative ego defense mechanisms as a solution can often lead to behaviors that would be categorized as highly dysfunctional, sometimes illegal, and often immoral. But it's important to remember that although the behaviors are the outcome, and often become the source of new and destructive behaviors, they are still not considered the original source!

For example, a person that has no coping strategy or skills for intense emotional pain may use alcohol for relief. If this becomes the coping skill alcoholism might result, which leads to a host of other issues.

These defense mechanisms are generally used subconsciously to avoid a healthy grief and loss process, which is necessary to effectively deal with loss in a positive way and come out of the pain a stronger, healthier, more substantive person.

We use defense mechanisms because we don't want to deal with the problem, don't know how to deal with the problem, don't have the necessary resources, or we don't want to recognize or admit the need to elicit divine help.

We will take a more in-depth look at these defense mechanisms, as well as the healthy grief and loss process, in more detail in Chapter 5.

The Book of Job

Grief, loss, and change are no small matters—whether they're currently present in our lives or in the lives of others. The big question is then: How do we help our loved ones and ourselves?

Let's look at a classic example. In the book of Job, we see a man who, short of Jesus himself, endured just about the highest degree of loss in known history. He lost it all: his entire family (other than his wife) and everything he had. They were all good things, but God allowed them to be removed from his life. Job went from God-following prince to God-following pauper in a dramatically short time. In this story, we see examples of how to effectively manage grief, as well as how not to manage grief. We have in the book of Job such a poignant example of human capacity:

> Three of Job's friends heard of all the trouble that had fallen on him. Each traveled from his own country—Eliphaz from Teman, Bildad from Shuhah, Zophar from Naamath—and went together to Job to keep him company and comfort him. When they first caught sight of him, they couldn't believe what they saw—they hardly recognized him! They cried out in lament, ripped their robes, and dumped dirt on their heads as a sign of their grief. Then they sat with him on the ground. Seven days and nights they sat there without saying a word. They could see how rotten he felt, how deeply he was suffering. (Job 2:11-13 MSG)

As the book progresses, we see a story of intense suffering and mediocre friendship (although his friends would not agree with that descriptor). His friends, who started out so nobly and appropriately by just sitting with him in his pain and saying nothing, eventually turned to various negative behaviors as they attempted to "help" Job process his loss. They began to talk: they consoled, they blamed, they problem-solved. These men, and Job's wife, turned to common defense mechanisms (avoidance, control, aggression, manipulation, etc.) to deal with this massive grief. A week later, of the four men, only Job himself handled his grief in a healthy way!

Yikes! Yet many of us would do the same thing. Sorrow is one of God's specialties, but it is not inherently ours. We all need God's guidance and the Holy Spirit's direction when helping others or ourselves through the process of suffering. And at the same time, when we're dealing with another person's suffering, we need to realize that we don't fully understand our friends' problems. We can't. It's between them and God.

We must remember that God did not comfort us to make us comfortable. He comforted us so that we may comfort others. We don't want to be like Job's friends, either to others or ourselves. One of the things we want to learn from Job's story is the importance of maintaining our own relationship with God. In fact, the best gift we can offer others and ourselves is that of knowing the source of all comfort and safety. When we press into God we can offer long-suffering, grace, and mercy. If we rely on our own resources, we will run out of mercy and grace, and we will then be left with unhelpful solutions, advice, and criticism. All very human solutions! We must respect the ministry of suffering and the dignity that transcends this process.

As it was, no good would have come from this situation had Job not stayed the course. He neither tried to change things nor blamed God—he simply grieved. It's worth noting that Job's wife had experienced the same abundance (family, wealth, success) that God had given Job, but when it came to suffering and loss, she was willing to walk away from her faith and encouraged Job to do the same. But Job so aptly says in Job 13:15, "Though he slay me, yet will I hope in him; I will surely defend my ways to his face" (NIV). I doubt Job could have conceived of anything good, and certainly not superior, coming from his loss. Just think of the impact his life has had on Christians and non-Christians alike for thousands of years now. He had no way of knowing the impact of his own story; he just had to live it! When seasons end, people pass, things are lost, and dreams die, it is very difficult to trust that God can still bring better.

Looking more deeply at Job and his wife, we see that they experienced, together, the same atrocious tragedies. It's important to note that their reactive behaviors were somewhat similar in fashion, but opposite in attitude. The difference was trust. Job never lost sight of who God was, and he continued to accept that God is God. "Acceptance, the key to all my problems," reads the Big Book from AA. He went through the entire grief and loss process honestly, authentically, and deeply without blaming or apologizing for his grief and loss. He felt shock, went through denial, tried bargaining, and was angry to the point that he cursed the day he was born (but important to note: he did not curse God). He then endured tremendous mourning to finally accept what had happened and found peace, only to be rewarded by God with far more than he had lost.

> *Acceptance, the key to all my problems.*
> *- A.A. Big Book*

Interestingly, Job's wife, who reacted with none of Job's positive attitudes and behaviors, is conspicuously absent from the happy ending we see at the end of the book. Although she escaped death, she was not mentioned in the last scene, which describes the abundance of all that God restored to Job. Had Job's wife become too embittered, too cynical, and too skeptical of what God restored? Job became stronger, wiser, closer to God, and more prosperous as a result of his ordeal, and his wife, perhaps graciously, was not mentioned.

This begs the question: How *should* I deal with changes, suffering, and subsequent pain? Here are a few suggestions:

1. *Go with the flow.* Don't try to "change the change." Remember: "Acceptance, the key to all my problems."
2. *Accept your feelings.* Do not judge your feelings. They are neither right nor wrong, good nor bad; they just are. We must *judiciously* judge our actions. This allows for appropriate resolution through the grief and loss process.
3. *Communicate your feelings* in whatever form is best for you (verbally, writing/journaling, artwork, physically, anything without negative destruction, etc.).
4. *Seek support if you need it.* You may need to seek support from friends, family, or professionals (for example: therapists, life coaches, sponsors, mentors, doctors, lawyers, pastors, etc.)—whoever is helpful to you.
5. *Take care of you.* Be healthy. Grieving and change are exhausting.
6. *Focus on the gains.*
7. *Address and strengthen your spiritual life.*
8. *Pray for wisdom, healing, and vision.*

Accepting change can be a burdensome task, but

it's vital for growth and an abundant life. In most cases, this first type of death is the third type of change—one that is inevitable and unavoidable. If I resist it and try to avoid it, the person I was truly intended to be will die! For example, if I am later in life, I may have to experience more death. This may be due to the fact that I am moving from the middle to the older generation. It's an inevitable and unavoidable change, but sad nonetheless. Along with it will come the inevitable and unavoidable change of menopause, impotency, and the decline of my body. The question then becomes, "Am I willing to go through the grief and loss process in order to deal with these changes appropriately? Furthermore, am I willing to allow myself the opportunity to enjoy an abundant life regardless of the life stage or circumstances I may find myself in?"

Essentially, are you prepared to allow God to use these changes so that life will abound?

Reflection Questions:

1. How relevant is this information to your current life situation? Are there changes you've been resisting that God might be trying to use for you? Do you recognize the difference between

self-will, free will, and God's will? How are they playing out, or being revealed, in your life?

2. Think back through your life: how have you usually responded to change? Can you identify any defense mechanisms? Can you remember any changes you allowed that produced good, even if the good happened years into the future?

3. Think of a change you're working through (positively or negatively). List some things that you could do to help yourself face it with a more positive response. Pick one, and make it a goal to do it this week.

4. Picture yourself facing a change positively. What would it look like? List some possible positive outcomes. Pray that God will use a change in your life to bring abundance in His own way.

5. When did you experience a transition and subsequent loss that you *did not* accept, or handle, properly? What consequences are you still incurring because of your resistance to accepting this loss? What were some of the "takeaways"? In other words, what did God

reveal to you about *you* in how you reacted or responded to this event?

6. What are the emotions you are currently experiencing, or have experienced, because it?

7. How have you reacted negatively to inevitable changes, such as marriage, middle years, mature years, empty nest, loss of status, change in health/aging, finances, relationship changes, or what may be relevant to you?

8. Are you resisting the change, or are you trying to "change the change"? What does *acceptance, the key to all my problems* mean to you? What feelings are evoked in you as you consider the need to *accept*?

9. Are you accepting of your feelings? Do you need to forgive yourself? Are you judging yourself? Are you willing to go through the grief and loss process?

10. Are you willing to communicate your feelings? What are you doing to communicate your feelings in a healthy way?

11. What type of support do you need to elicit as you go through this process?

12. How willing are you to take care of *you*? What do you need? Is it better eating habits, more sleep, or more appropriate expectations of yourself, etc.? Focus on the gains.

13. How are you addressing your spiritual life? What are your feelings toward God? If they are negative, are you accepting of them and willing to talk with God about it? Remember: He wants all of us, even the negative parts of us.

14. Are you praying for wisdom, healing, and vision? Are you willing to ask another to pray for you regarding these needs?

Chapter 3

THE DEATH OF THE THING THAT IS KILLING ME

Because anyone who has died has been set free from sin. (Romans 6:7 NIV)

"The cure of death is dying." (C.S. Lewis) [5]

Could it be any clearer? Our old way of life was nailed to the cross with Christ, a decisive end to that sin-miserable life—no longer at sin's every beck and call! What we believe is this: If we get included in Christ's sin-conquering death, we also get included in his life-saving resurrection. We know that when Jesus was raised from the dead it was a signal of the end of death-as-the-end. Never again will death have the last word. When Jesus died, he took sin down with him, but alive he brings God down to us. From now on, think of it this way: Sin speaks a dead language that means nothing to you; God speaks your mother tongue, and you hang on every word. You are dead to sin and alive to God. That's what Jesus did. (Romans 6:6–11 MSG)

A time to kill and a time to heal. A time to tear down and a time to build up. (Ecclesiastes 3:3 NLT)

As we found in the last chapter, we're often forced into the first type of death: an inevitable, unavoidable, oftentimes unexpected change. How we respond is key. But with the second type of death—the death of the thing that is killing me—we might be in for a

If you don't do the internal work, the external won't work.

slow, lifelong change process from the inside out. The "thing" may have seeped into our lives, influenced by a variety of factors from childhood and beyond, and is now such an ordinary part of life that we barely notice it. It's tricky that way. The first type hits us like a blunt force; the second acts more like a slow-working poison or debilitating disease.

The second type of death might be anything from a character flaw to a sin from our past that still has a hold on us, to a relationship that's impacting us negatively. It's generally a "sin" issue that, if denied, rationalized, or otherwise left unattended to, will manifest itself as a character issue. It might be an addiction, a vice, a habit, or a way of life. We might need to die to overeating, to pornography, to an over-busy lifestyle that leaves no time for prayer. On the other hand, the "thing" might be something that was once good, but that is now stifling who we're meant to be. It could be a hobby, career or relationship that can no longer coexist with God's plan for our lives or a mindset that doesn't seem harmful, but is stunting our growth nonetheless. It's usually a sin issue—something we're not letting go of, or correcting, that we're supposed to deal with. This can happen when we refuse to let a good thing die for the better thing. It starts as the first type of death (a change) but turns into the second type: the thing that is killing me. Resisting the first type of death and not allowing a healthy grief and loss process gives rise to unhealthy defense mechanisms and self-medicating behavior. These may manifest themselves in addictions, compulsive/impulsive behaviors and a whole host of sins.

When considering the second kind of death, it's important to first understand how sin and death entered the world in the first place. Think back to Adam and Eve. When they made that fateful choice, they decided that their way, not God's way, was the right way. They invited death into the world by shattering their own innocence and the will of the Life-Giver. Death abounded—all of a sudden, man's relationship with his Creator was broken, timelessness had come to an end, man's destiny was thwarted, and the earthly bodies of humankind, too, would die. In fact, the whole of creation is dying as you read this.

And it would take more death to remedy the situation. It's odd, isn't it, how God's plans often oppose the way we think? But it makes sense: naturally, God would do the opposite of what our fallen minds would create as "the solution" to our problems. Throughout the Old Testament we see death making up for wrong choices—not only through endless sacrifices for sin, but also as a consequence, sometimes in grand scale, for refusing to submit to God. God is so very creative in the way He uses death to teach, purify, and bring new life. Take a moment and read the following passage from the book of Numbers the twenty-first chapter:

> And the Israelites set out again. They left Mount Hor and traveled by way of the Red Sea, skirting Edom; but again, the difficult travel gave everyone a short temper. [5] They challenged both God and Moses.
>
> **Israelites:** What were you thinking to bring us up out of Egypt and let us die out here in this desert land? There's nothing to eat and no water either. We are sick and tired of living on what food we have.

> As a divine response, the Eternal One sent venomous snakes among them and the people were bitten. A number of Israelites were indeed killed by them. They then appealed to Moses.
>
> **Israelites:** We are so sorry! We know that it was wrong to speak against the Eternal and against you. Please talk to the Him, and get Him to take these awful snakes away. So Moses appealed to God on behalf of the terrified and chastened congregation, and He instructed Moses.
>
> **Eternal One:** Make a venomous snake that looks like the ones tormenting the congregation, and put it on a pole. Everyone who gets bitten can simply look at your serpent and be healed. (Numbers 21:4-8 VOICE)

We see in this passage a reference to some of the character issues needing to die in the lives of the wandering Israelites. Starting in verse four we see that they became short-tempered (the NIV version says they grew impatient), challenged, and spoke against both God and Moses by complaining about the food and water. Furthermore, and far more egregious, the people actually accused both God and Moses of "not thinking," that they have "now brought them out into the desert just to die." As a result, their sin begins to lead to death. God's *divine response* is to send venomous snakes that cause many to be sick when bitten and even kill some of the accusing complainers. We know that "sin leads to death," and due to this consequence, the people "come to their senses" and realize their mistake. They appeal to

Moses and say they are sorry, as well as asking for the death snakes to be taken away. Moses appeals to God on behalf of these frightened and humbled people.

God's solution is very creative. He tells Moses to make a venomous snake that "looks like" the snakes tormenting the people and hang it on a pole. The notes regarding these verses in the *Ryrie Study Bible* indicate that if the people looked on the bronze snake and believed in God, they lived. Furthermore, the New Testament cites this instance as an example of Jesus' death on the cross and personal faith being a necessity for salvation. God is already setting the stage for all of us—that is, seeing how our character issues bring death when we don't repent from them. We must acknowledge the thing that brings death to us—whether it is our impatience and unwillingness to trust "God's Ways" (like the Israelites) or some other issue which may be causing us to miss out on the abundant life. Whatever it may be, God is showing us that when we are genuinely sorry, and truly believe in Him (Christ is the anti-venom), we must then ***look*** at the thing that is killing us. When we do, it is then that we heal completely and live! "*And as Moses lifted up the serpent in the wilderness, even so must the Son of Man be lifted up, that whoever believes in Him should not perish but have eternal life*" (John 3:14-15 NKJV).

Wow, how it changes in the New Testament! This is the Good News!! When Jesus became the sacrifice, once for all, death no longer had any hold on creation.

As a result of Adam's choice, God needed to conquer death *through death* in order to bring life back into His creation. How could Adam's choice be so significant? Adam chose his own will, self-will, instead of *God's will*. Our way brings death eternal; God's way brings life eternal. The sin of using free will to choose self-will over God's will has put us on a very painful trajectory. The only way to break free is to use our free will to die to self-will, choose God's will, and then to allow God's way to permeate our lives. Death is the problem, but it's also the solution. This means identifying and ridding ourselves of everything that's holding us captive.

The tricky thing about discovering your captor is that it can masquerade as something good. This means that something that is part of *someone else's* abundant life may not be part of yours. Consider 1 Corinthians 10:23: *Everything is permissible, but not everything is constructive* (ISV/NIV). What a struggle this can be to understand and accept, both in ourselves and in others! Personally, I love cigarettes. Does that surprise you? It should: I haven't smoked since 1985. I had just graduated from college and was moving to Los Angeles to work in the buying offices for Robinson's/May (now known as Macy's). Smoking was already affecting my singing voice, and I didn't want it to get in the way of my future. I knew that if I didn't quit then, I would most likely smoke the rest of my life. Quitting is one of the hardest things I've ever done. I never want to have to go through that again. And, unlike many people I know who can enjoy one cigarette, or cigar, or pipe, I can never smoke again! One cigarette would quickly bring me back up to the pack a day I was smoking as a 22-year-old. That's how addictions work: they lay dormant until they're awakened, and then they return in full force.

I do not believe there's anything inherently wrong with smoking for many people. But for me? It has to be off-limits. It's *permissible* for me, but it's certainly not *constructive* for me. In fact, it's detrimental because it reignites a very powerful addiction back into my life. This isn't legalism, but it is something I need to respect about myself. The knowledge that I will never smoke again is wisdom about myself that God has given me, and it's self-care. Smoking had once been my captor, but it is no longer allowed access to me because of my free will. I use my free will to combat my self-will, thus remaining free from an addiction to cigarettes.

Your captor could also be that something that's

been a part of God's plan for you in the past but will not be a part of your future. I've walked this out in a very personal way while writing this book. I'll confess: I was rather addicted to paper, as opposed to electronics. I resisted computers, e-mail, online banking, and all the rest—to the point that it would've hampered my ministry had God not stepped in and *suggested* I launch into the twenty-first century. My previous systems had worked before, but they weren't right for my life going forward. I could have let this be the first type of death, the "death of good thing for the better," but I hung on and resisted! Despite my discomfort with all things electronic, and the fact that I liked my old systems and did not *want* to change, I obeyed.

I realized I needed to change my attitude about technology and stop resisting all the really beneficial things about it. If I didn't, I would kill all the plans God had for my ministry and the manifestation of my calling. But it wasn't smooth sailing from there; apparently I refused to "die" to this love of paper soon enough. God waited, and then His timing kicked in! A massive computer crash later, and I found myself becoming a veritable expert—completely against my will, mind you!—in my particular brand of computer. There was lots of pain, but lots of gain, too. And I can already see how God is going to use this as I continue my work.

My avoidance of technology needed to die and, just as we saw in the analogy of the seed, we need to allow growth, change, and metamorphosis. With this second type of death, we do so *voluntarily*. We surrender our will to God's will and allow Him to guide us through the process of giving up and letting go. I was initially unwilling to grow and resistant to change, but I finally, begrudgingly, decided to allow the change. I voluntarily gave in and took the plunge, only after some really big life *encouragements,* e.g. my computer crashing and almost losing this entire book. For me, this represented both types of death. Through God's mercy and patience He not only guided me, but brought me safely through. I can now consider myself officially "wired."

We need to go through this dying process for whatever bogs us down, whatever holds us, whatever has power over us, and whatever is in control of us; anything that has made itself bigger or more important than God has to die. Some things have to die because they are harmful and destructive. These things will steal, kill, or otherwise destroy our ability to be that "best version" of ourselves. This is different from the good things that have to "die away," not because they were bad or destructive, but because their purpose or time is over. And if I don't allow for the natural dying process, then the thing that was once appropriate and necessary to my life will kill or destroy me. The good thing that originally allowed healthy development now impedes the natural developmental process. Think back to the caterpillar: If it were to never leave the cocoon, it would never become what it was truly intended to be; subsequently, the lovely caterpillar will surely die within that wonderful cocoon, without reaching its true potential. That's a tragedy twice over, and one we don't have to experience if we allow the second type of death to take place: the death of the thing that is holding me captive.

Love Never Fails. Never. *Really.*

If you allow Him, God will make the necessary adjustments to your life that will lead you to His version of abundance for you, including unhitching you from anything, positive or negative, that's holding you back from your new life. The key is to surrender your self-will to God's will. And our challenge, as we uncovered in Chapter 1, is that His plan will probably make little sense to us; it will be completely different from what we'd do. Not only will we have difficulty comprehending what in the world He's doing, it will most likely test our faith, our confidence, and even our understanding of our own sanity. We'll feel out of control, a bit (or a lot) lost, and quite uncomfortable.

Due to the fact that we may not recognize "God's way," we may feel abandoned and neglected, while He is, in fact, completing the good work in us. It might help you to remind yourself in this process that He doesn't think the way we think, and He doesn't work the way we work. Thank God! Because my ways certainly don't seem to be working, and my thoughts, no matter how intelligent I think I may be, certainly don't seem to be very smart sometimes—actually much of the time, honestly speaking.

Plant the following passage from Isaiah in your mind, and reference it often as you let God work:

> Let's see what they have to say about this, how they account for what's happened. Let them present their expert witnesses and make their case; let them try to convince us what they say is true. "But you are my witnesses." God's Decree: "You're my handpicked servant, so that you'll come to know and trust me, understand both that I am and who I am. Previous to me there was no such thing as a god, nor will there be after me. I, yes I, am God. I'm the only Savior there is. I spoke, I saved, I told you what existed long before these upstart gods appeared on the scene. And you know it, you're my witnesses, you're

the evidence." God's Decree: "Yes, I am God. I've always been God and I always will be God. No one can take anything from me. **I make; who can unmake it?**" (Isaiah 43:10-13 MSG, emphasis added)

The NIV version reminds me that "when God's hand acts, no man can reverse it." How comforting this is to me to know that "if God changed it, God sustains it" because I know that many changes we make don't always seem to stick. I only have to say "diet" and "holidays," and you'll know what I mean.

I like how emphatically God expresses Himself. Not only is He God, the only real God, but what He makes, no one can unmake; what He does, no man can reverse. When you surrender to God's way, and He takes you through a dying process, it's final; nothing on earth can change the new work God has done in you. You're permanently changed. Now, you're not permanently *perfect*, however, or invincible. It's certainly possible to pick up a new dysfunction or take the growth process in a horizontal direction, but you can't undo what God has already done in your life. Thank God!

If God changed it, God sustains it.

What are "His ways"? What are "His thoughts"?

How does a father think toward a child? As we address our character issues, our fleshly desires, and simply, our sin, we see clearly through Scripture how God feels about us and how He is able to deal with us, because of the death of Jesus. Namely, whatever sin we have, resulting in bondage or captivity, is always addressed under the auspice of love. Satan, on the other hand, wants you to believe that God addresses the bondage you're in, whether it is a trauma response, or self-imposed bondage, through the auspice of law. The short version is, "God addresses our sin through love; Satan attacks our sin through the law." That is why it feels so condemning, why we feel so far from God. Whereas, when God addresses my sin, although it may hurt and be uncomfortable, I always feel closer to God. I am inspired through the hope that I know will not disappoint me, the hope I have in the redeeming love offered through Christ's death. If Satan manages to convince you that God cannot love you, and in fact abhors you, he will be able to keep you in bondage forever. Let's see what God has to say:

> The Lord hears the needy and does not despise his captive people. (Psalm 69:33 NIV)

> For God listens to the poor, He doesn't walk out on the wretched. (Psalm 69:33 MSG)

But now, this is what the Lord says—he who created you, Jacob, he who formed you, Israel: "Do not fear, for I have redeemed you; I have summoned you by name; you are mine." (Isaiah 43:1 NIV)

God wants you to know that He is faithful when He says, "There is therefore no condemnation for those who are in Christ Jesus" (Romans 8:1 NKJV). The Message Bible says, "We no longer have to live under a continuous low-lying black cloud; a new power is in operation." We know this new power to be the power of love. We see this in the famous "love chapter." Did you ever stop to think that when we read the love chapter at weddings, God's not just handing down instructions? No, He's expressing *first* how He feels about us and then asking us to do the same for ourselves so that we have a God-supply of love to give to others. Remember, love never fails. This is the way God loved us when He sent His perfect Son to die for us. In fact, this is the way Jesus loved us when He submitted to his fate. When you

> *"Do not fear, for I have redeemed you; I have summoned you by name; you are mine."*
> *Isaiah 43:1 NIV*

read 1 Corinthians 13, read it as if it is God talking to you about how He is loving you, not simply as an edict for how you are to love.

What's more, He's telling us how He wants us to love ourselves. I'm frequently asked, "Why is it so hard for me to like myself?" That's because we all think we know ourselves and that the person we see is the "real" us. I know how it feels; there have been times in my life when I've just wanted to "unzip" myself and crawl out. The truth is, if we were truly able to see ourselves as God sees us, we would have no trouble liking and even loving ourselves. Think of the people you love, especially children. We know all of the irritating, frustrating, and even disgusting things they do or say, but we also see past that to who they "really" are. God does this in a much deeper, more profound way—a way that is based in truth *and* love, not just love. He sees who we really are: our perfect, resurrected self, and He is pleased! He sees through the eyes of love, through the eyes of Jesus. Only when we begin to see how God loves us, can we love others and ourselves.

God *is* Love, so when God is being himself, He is saying to us in the famous "love chapter"
(1 Corinthians 13:3-8 MSG, paraphrase):
"I" never give up.
"I" care more for others than for myself.

"My" love doesn't want what it doesn't have.

"My" love doesn't strut,

"I" don't have a swelled head,

"I" don't force myself on you

"I" don't say, "Me first,"

"I" don't fly off the handle,

"I" don't keep score of the sins of others (your sins),

"I" don't revel when (you) or others grovel,

"I" don't take pleasure in the flowering of truth,

"I" put up with anything,

"I" trust God always,

"I" always look for the best,

"I" never look back

"I" keep going to the end.

Love never dies.

Love never dies, love never fails—this is God being God to us.

It is God's love for us.

It has taken me years to come to grips with the fact that I was a "legalist." I wanted to believe I was a grace-based person, but I'm not, or at least, I haven't been. God's working with me on it, teaching me that it's all about love, and love never fails. I came to learn the "love chapter" on a very different level when God revealed to me that this is the way He loves me. Imagine how humbling it was for me to see this! This revelation to me was more important than simply showing me how I was to love others; after all, how can we love others with God's love if we're not really receiving it ourselves? I needed this type of love to face my character flaws and subsequent sins. So the Lord beautifully showed me Isaiah 43:18–19:

> Forget the former things; do not dwell on the past. See, I am doing a new thing! Now it springs up; do you not perceive it? I am making a way in the wilderness and streams in the wasteland. (Isaiah 43:18–19 NIV)

How sweet, how kind, that God would address all my sin through the eyes of love, and then tell me to "forget about it"! It is not in a way that makes it meaningless, or no big deal, or in any way okay; God takes our sin very seriously because sin causes death, and God hates death. He is simply saying the past has already occurred, but there's no reason for it to have a hold on us or to keep us in bondage. Instead, we can repent, leave it behind, and look forward! We see time and time again throughout the Bible that forgiveness and acceptance always follow repentance. God doesn't make us anguish for long. It's not that our past can't help us, but the only thing we can productively do now about our past is to learn from it, using it with God's help, in the process of becoming a new creation. In fact, if we don't learn from it, we have "pain in vain" instead of learning from it and having our pain be for gain. Remember, the ability to retrospect was never intended for self-abuse, it was only intended for us to learn and to see how far we have come. If we use it for self-loathing and abuse, the toxic shame that results from that will more often than not cause us to make the same foolish mistakes again. But once we've taken what we can from the past, it's imperative that we consider it what it truly is—old history!

Perhaps we're longing for a past season, one filled with joy, hope, and prosperity that has come and gone. Nevertheless, if we're looking back to do more than simply thank God, or to learn, we're still in bondage. Lot's wife, for example, longed for Sodom and her old life when God wanted to give her a "better" life, a healthier life, and more meaningful, godly life. He wanted to give her a life that allowed her to fulfill her purpose, to walk out her calling, and to be whom she was created to be in the first place. But she looked back, and she died. Anything that keeps us from living in the "here and now" keeps us from being present in what God is doing and will make us "dead."

No matter how good our past was, and regardless of how bad it was, God says, "I'm doing a new thing—Don't you see it!?" (Isaiah 43:18–19 NLT).

No matter what has happened or what we've done, the past does not have to separate us from the love of God. But it still can, if we let it. Look at Romans 8:35–39:

> Who shall separate us from the love of Christ? Shall trouble or hardship or persecution or famine or nakedness or danger or sword? As it is written: "For your sake we face death all day long; we are considered as sheep to be slaughtered." No, in all these things we are more than conquerors through him who loved us. For I am convinced that neither death nor life, neither angels nor demons, neither the present nor the future, nor any powers, neither height nor depth, nor anything else in all creation, will be able to separate us from the love of God that is in Christ Jesus our Lord. (NIV)

None of these things will be able to separate us from the love of God. In the reference to "neither the present nor the future," however, we do not see the *past*. Our past *can* separate us from the *experience* of God's love, if we let it. It will not separate us from the truth that God loves us, but it can separate us but from enjoying it, living in it, and being filled with it. He still loves us, but our past can keep us from knowing it, if we let it.

Most often, our being unable to escape our past is due to our own self-condemnation. We feel like it's both necessary and legitimate to condemn ourselves. And yet, in Romans 8:1–2 (MSG), we learn that we're not supposed to be our own judge and jury. Take a look:

With the arrival of Jesus, the Messiah, that fateful dilemma is resolved. Those who enter into Christ's being-here-for-us no longer have to live under a continuous, low-lying black cloud. A new power is in operation. The Spirit of life in Christ, like a strong wind, has magnificently cleared the air, freeing you from a fated lifetime of brutal tyranny at the hands of sin and death.

God did not redeem me for what I could do, but for who I could be.

There are plenty of other verses that reassure us of the same truth: God loves us, we're forgiven, and we're free in Jesus. I've included them at the end of this chapter for your reference. The truth is, God is **dying** to redeem us. He wants us to be our best.

He knows it's possible. He has a way to make it happen. And He's ready to move forward—are you?

Let's look a little more closely at the dying, and redemption, process to see what God might have in store for all of us metaphorically. To do so, we'll visit a historical figure with a rather unique story: Lazarus.

Why Did Lazarus Have to Die?

Lazarus died. This is neither the end of the story, nor the beginning—yet, it is the story. We don't know what malady Lazarus was fighting, nor do we know precisely what God had for him after he was brought back to life; we only know that not only did he die, but he *had* to die to live out his true calling. There was no other way.

We can imagine the scene: Lazarus is sick, wasting away. He's fighting to stay alive. How long did he resist death? His family is helping him—tracking down the best doctors, selling possessions, perhaps, to buy expensive medicine, tending him through sleepless nights, and trying anything and everything that might be able to save his life. But no one, no matter how committed, could stop the dying process; nor could they cause him to have new life through this process. In fact, when all was said and done, they really weren't much help at all.

But we, whether we're in Lazarus' shoes or his family's shoes, would likely do no better. While it seems natural to resist death—and certainly there's no reason to let an injury or illness get the better of us if we can help it—how hard should we fight? There might be things living in us, for example, that aren't worth the fight we give them to keep them alive. What needs to die so I may fully live for Jesus, fulfilling His calling and His purpose on earth for me?

The dying process is ultimately one of acceptance. We must go through a grief and loss process that includes forgiveness (of ourselves, of others, maybe even of God) and recognizes and accepts mistakes made by others and ourselves in our lives. Let me elaborate a bit on forgiving God—after all, He does no wrong that needs to be forgiven—as well as forgiving friends and family who may not have done what we wanted, or may have responded in a corrective manner (for instance, set a boundary). Even though they did the right thing, we might feel disappointed or upset by their actions. While they didn't directly hurt us, we got hurt *on* them and aren't happy about it.

It's like running into a brick wall, getting a bloody nose, and then become distrusting of the wall. I got hurt on the wall; the wall didn't hurt me. In these cases, forgiveness is still an important part of the relationship. If I don't forgive the hurt that was caused, our relationship will suffer from resentment, walls, defensiveness, and lack of trust, lack of vulnerability, protectiveness, and more. We forgive God and people who were in the right because we got our feelings hurt *on* them, not necessarily *by* them.

It's interesting to me that in this story, only Jesus knew the truth. He knew that Lazarus' death was necessary, even fatal, but He also knew that it was not *permanent*. Everyone else, on the other hand, could not accept that Lazarus had to die, but they did believe his death would be fatal and therefore permanent. Jesus knew that Lazarus' death, although fatal, would not be permanent. He saw it as the process Lazarus needed to go through to become everything he needed to be and knew that it would ultimately give glory to God. This illustrates death of a dream. Although the death of a dream may be fatal, God's gifts and callings are irrevocable.

Romans 11:29 reminds us, "God's gifts and God's call are under full warranty—never cancelled, never rescinded" (MSG). In the NIV it says, "For God's gifts and his call are irrevocable." The death of our dream is permanent, but the calling is not. How kind our Lord is *again*, that our struggles and imperfections, as well as our deviations from His will, do not cancel out the call He has for our lives. They are the very reason that He created us.

This is why it's so important that we look for God's truth and His ways. We must integrate His thoughts, His love, His truth, His forgiveness. We must then integrate our repentance and our ultimate acceptance into this process of discovering what needs to die so that we may live.

The Bible is filled with examples regarding the need for something or someone to die in order for something or someone to live; but for today, let's focus on the encouraging story of Lazarus, along with the primary characters. Take note that God is a very efficient God; if He was doing a work in Lazarus, He was also at work in the hearts of everyone involved. As we go through this story, examining it in a metaphorical sense, think about which character(s) you most relate to. I could relate to them all in one way or another. Also, continue to consider what needs to die in order for you to live completely. I've taken the liberty of making parenthetical comments in the text to help guide your thought process. Feel free to allow God to show you how you might have reacted if you were there experiencing this event. (Please remember this is not meant as an exegetical commentary on the story of Lazarus. It is meant as a way to relate to what these characters may have been experiencing and, consequently, what this might show us about our own character and the process the Lord may be doing in each and every one of us).

THE CHARACTERS IN THE STORY:
God (present whether we perceive Him or not)
Jesus (primary character)
Lazarus (primary character)
Mary (sister of Lazarus)
Martha (sister of Lazarus)
The disciples (Jesus' friends and followers)
Thomas (a devout disciple and friend of Jesus)
The visiting Jews (the community at large)
The "others" among them (naysayers/community)

John 11:1-44 (MSG) The Death of Lazarus
A man was sick, Lazarus of Bethany, the town of Mary and her sister Martha. [*Are you sick with something, is there something killing you? Do you know that something needs to die, but find it hard to let go? What might Lazarus have been feeling or asking for? What might you have been saying or asking for? Have you felt unimportant to God, confused by your friendship with Him? Feeling that "in my greatest hour of need, God is not here"? Consider the faith Lazarus needed to*

practice, up until the very end. Was he trying to be strong for his sisters and those around him? Do you think he lost his faith and can you relate to the abandonment Lazarus may have felt? Imagine the difficulty he may have had as he continued to practice believing in Jesus when everything seemed so opposite. Maybe Lazarus was thinking, "Is Jesus really who He says He is?" or "I don't understand—He said he was my friend." It is also possible that Lazarus may have seen saying, "I deserve to die; I don't deserve to be healed." However he may have been languishing and saying to himself, "I wish I could die; I don't want to live, at least not like this!" Imagine the anguish and bewilderment he must have been feeling. Lastly, consider as well the impact on family, neighbors, coworkers, caregivers, doctors, etc. when a believer is facing death with faith! Are you one of those being affected? Or are you Lazarus, whom God wants to use to reveal His glory to those around you?] This was the same Mary who massaged the Lord's feet with aromatic oils and then wiped them with her hair. [*Have you practiced gestures that showed your deep and extravagant love for Jesus?*] It was her brother Lazarus who was sick. [*Have you done a great gesture of love for Jesus, all the while someone you love, or maybe even you, is sick?*] So the sisters sent word to Jesus, "Master, the one you love so very much is sick." [*Have you said to God, "The one you love is sick," or "The one I love is sick; please heal them," or "God, I am sick! Please come and heal me"?*]

When Jesus got the message, he said, "This sickness is not fatal. It will become an occasion to show God's glory by glorifying God's Son." [*Do you have the type of faith that seeks to glorify God even through trying circumstances? Take heart that God is not inflicting people with maladies so that He can use them; instead, believe that He's working with their condition to show His glory!*]

Jesus loved Martha and her sister and Lazarus [*Do you know you are loved by Jesus?*], but oddly [*"oddly" is the operative word here, because we must remember God's ways are not our ways. They may just appear "odd" to us*], when he heard that Lazarus was sick, he stayed on where he was for two more days. [*Have you felt like you waited on God, felt like He didn't care, that He had forgotten your dilemma, or that it wasn't that important to Him?*] After the two days, he said to his disciples, "Let's go back to Judea." [*Has God done something "odd"? Has He done things in an order or way that didn't make sense to you? Maybe He has been doing things in a way that would not have been "your way"?*]

They said, "Rabbi, you can't do that. The Jews

are out to kill you, and you're going back?" [*Have you been a disciple that wanted to protect or defend God? One that "cared" more about God than the ones He cares about?*]

Jesus replied, "Are there not twelve hours of daylight? Anyone who walks in daylight doesn't stumble because there's plenty of light from the sun. Walking at night, he might very well stumble because he can't see where he's going." [*Has the Lord ever responded to you in a way that makes no sense? As in, "I know that this is from God, but I have no idea what He is trying to tell me!"*]

He said these things, and then announced, "Our friend Lazarus has fallen asleep. I'm going to wake him up."

The disciples said, "Master, if he's gone to sleep, he'll get a good rest and wake up feeling fine." [*Have you been the follower that went "literal" on God and ended up missing the point completely, minimizing a very serious issue?*] Jesus was talking about death, while his disciples thought he was talking about taking a nap.

Then Jesus became explicit: "Lazarus died. [*Don't we all need God to be this blunt with us?*] And I am glad for your sakes that I wasn't there. You're about to be given new grounds for believing. [*Are you willing to accept that God may be "glad" when something is painful because it will lead to a deeper belief? Have you asked the Lord to increase your faith, your knowledge of Him, and your understanding of Him, only to incur a trial?*] Now let's go to him." [*Are you willing to accept God's timing? Previously he waited (oddly), and then His voice says, "Now."*]

That's when Thomas, the one called the Twin, said to his companions, "Come along. We might as well die with him." [*Have you ever "flip-flopped" when previously taking God literally, then trying to be "deep" and pious, then still missing the point entirely? When Thomas actually did understand that he needed to die (just not permanently!), he could still only think in physical terms.*]

When Jesus finally got there, he found Lazarus already four days dead. Bethany was near Jerusalem, only a couple of miles away, and many of the Jews were visiting Martha and Mary, sympathizing with them over their brother [*Have you been there for someone while they were enduring a trial? What did God impress upon you?*]. Martha heard Jesus was coming and went out to meet him. Mary remained in the house.

Martha said, "Master, if you'd been here, my brother wouldn't have died. Even now, I know that whatever you ask God he will give you." [*Have you ever told God what you really thought and then tried to make it sound spiritual or tried to make it sound right?*]

Jesus said, "Your brother will be raised up."

Martha replied, "I know that he will be raised up in the resurrection at the end of time." [*Have you continued to be "religious," missing it when God is being literal, and subsequently not interacting with God in the "now"? Martha is really trying here—sometimes we all feel like we are on the "other side" of God's point. Martha had knowledge, but she was struggling with understanding. The whole dying process is about growing knowledge into understanding, at which point we can begin to uncover and employ wisdom. You are not alone in this; we are not born with wisdom. It takes experience to see what Jesus really can do. For those of us who often feel "in the dark," remember that God knows we are struggling and, in fact, He is well aware that we are not God!*]

"You don't have to wait for the End. I am, right now, Resurrection and Life. The one who believes in me, even though he or she dies, will live. And everyone who lives believing in me does not ultimately die at all. Do you believe this?" [*Is God saying this to you: "If you die, you will live."?*] "Do you believe I am the Way?" [*These two verses are the point of the entire story!*]

"Yes, Master. All along I have believed that you are the Messiah, the Son of God who comes into the world." [*Have you ever continued to practice your faith in a circumstance that is so painful and makes no sense to you at all spiritually and naturally? Martha gets it right!*]

After saying this, she went to her sister Mary and whispered in her ear [*After we are humbled, we are often kinder and gentler to others*], "The Teacher is here and is asking for you."

The moment she heard that, she jumped up and ran out to him. [*Are you willing to run to Jesus in the midst of a circumstance that seems so wrong, so contradictory to what God can do?*] Jesus had not yet entered the town but was still at the place where Martha had met him. When her sympathizing Jewish friends saw Mary run off, they followed her, thinking she was on her way to the tomb to weep there. [*Have you ever wondered what God was doing, desperate to see something miraculous? Have you been willing and wanting to follow it wherever it may be? Have you wanted to believe that God would do something for the one you loved and desired to be of service to the people afflicted?*] Mary came to where Jesus was waiting and fell at his feet, saying, "Master, if only you had been here, my brother would not have died." [*Have you been willing to be honest with Jesus and not just say the religious thing but, instead, to be truly relational with*

Him about your circumstance and your responses?]

When Jesus saw her sobbing and the Jews with her sobbing, a deep anger welled up within him. [*Have you ever felt angry with people, or yourself, because we struggle to trust him? Have you ever put God in a box? Have you ever been in pain because you didn't trust His ways? Jesus knew if people really knew Him they would trust Him and would not have to experience such painful feelings. Did you know that Jesus is deeply saddened and angered by sickness and death? But even so, He knows that much better things are coming, and that the more we trust Him, the less intensely these feelings of grief and sorrow will pain us.*] He said, "Where did you put him?" [*Has Jesus heard your cries without addressing your pain, and the circumstance continued? It's interesting here that Jesus didn't address their pain but instead kept on with his plan.*]

"Master, come and see," they said. Now Jesus wept. [*Are you like Jesus and willing to weep when you realize people's fragility and humanness, feeling compassion instead of judgment?*]

The Jews said, "Look how deeply he loved him." [*Do you then realize the depth of love God has for his people?*]

Others among them said, "Well, if he loved him so much, why didn't he do something to keep him from dying? After all, he opened the eyes of a blind man." [*Or, in contrast, have you been one of the skeptics and critics about how God chooses to act? Subsequently using Scripture and "facts" to justify why you think God "dropped the ball"? Do you criticize and scoff at the way God does things because you don't understand? Have you ever said out loud, or in your heart, "If He really is who He says He is, then...(this or that, etc.)"? This is Antichrist thinking. This is the very tone and tack Satan used in the Garden*]

Then Jesus, the anger again welling up within him, arrived at the tomb. [*Do you become appropriately frustrated when people relegate God to their way, their thoughts, and use His past works against Him?*] It was a simple cave in the hillside with a slab of stone laid against it. Jesus said, "Remove the stone." [*Are you willing to help roll away another person's "stone"?*]

The sister of the dead man, Martha, said, "Master, by this time there's a stench. He's been dead four days!" [*Have you ever said, "But God, you don't understand what you are saying or what you are asking," again responding to God through our experiences, our intellect, and what makes sense to us? As if Jesus didn't know this?*]

Jesus looked her in the eye. "Didn't I tell you that if you believed, you would see the glory of God?"

[*Have you ever felt rebuked by God? You see here that He didn't address the initial complaint or challenge; instead He focused them on a higher truth about who He is.*]

Then, to the others, "Go ahead, take away the stone." [*We see here that the ones He originally asked to roll away the stone did not do it. As a result, He had to go to another group of people within the community. Have you been one of the people that were asked by God to do something, and you baulked, so He had to ask "others" while you were relegated to the viewing section? Have you been one of "the others" that were asked to do something because the original people didn't do what they were initially asked to do? Have you ever resented the fact that you were the "pinch hitter" or the second pick? Have you been a person that doubted what God was asking you to do, or have you ever argued with God about what He was asking you to do? Have you missed out on an opportunity to help another person heal because you didn't like the way it was being done? Maybe you have experienced God going to others to get His job done?*]

They removed the stone. [*Were you grateful to be asked or offended that He didn't go to you first?*] Jesus raised his eyes to heaven and prayed, "Father, I'm grateful that you have listened to me. I know you always do listen, but on account of this crowd standing here I've spoken so that they might believe that you sent me." [*Jesus is role modeling for us how to believe about His father. Are you willing to follow the lead of Jesus?*]

Then he shouted, "Lazarus, come out!" [*Has God asked you to "come out"? Does He need to shout? Has He asked you to come out and be "you," to come out and speak the truth, whether that is some type of confession of faith or a confession of repentance? Is He shouting at you to take responsibility for something, or to act with courage and confidence regarding your faith? What is God asking you to come forth and do, say, act, or renounce? Remember His "raised voice/shout" is one of authority and confidence for us; He did not shout "at him" or in anger.*] And he came out, a cadaver, wrapped from head to toe, and with a kerchief over his face. [*Did you "come out"? Are you willing to come out looking ugly, stinky, wrapped up, tangled up, and in bondage?*] Jesus told them, "Unwrap him and let him loose." [*Are you willing to be one of those who unwraps, unties, or removes the grave clothes of the ugly, stinky person, even if you are one of the ones that wrapped the person up to begin with? Are you willing to be unwrapped, untied, and actually helped because you can't do it yourself? Imagine if Lazarus rejected help and tried to get himself unbound? I think we often look* that way; we are wrestling, rolling around, trying desperately to get free when God has people all around us to provide help and support. Jesus did not ask him to come forth until He had everything in place: all the help and appropriate support Lazarus needed. Jesus made sure "the stage was set" in a way that ensured Lazarus' success.]

Did you find yourself in the story of Lazarus? Maybe you typically see yourself as part of the crowd—the "others," watching a story unfold, sometimes participating, hoping for a miracle but not necessarily understanding it. Maybe you're a disciple who has trouble seeing the truth, even if it's right in front of you. Or maybe you're Mary, running to Jesus and being completely honest about what's in your heart. I'd like to suggest that we all may share something with Lazarus: needing to come forth. Note that he had to do this on his own; other people could roll away the stone and untie him, but he had to make the move when the time was right. When he was **called,** he had to get up and come forward.

> *"Waiting exercises our grace; waiting tries our faith; therefore, wait on in hope; for though the promise tarry, it can never come too late."*
> *– C. H. Spurgeon.*

There is a time to kill and a time to heal. Some things need to die; some things need to be fixed. This is the delicate balance that God has laid out for us. Alongside killing comes allowing to die, but there is a slight difference. Killing is more active; it takes our willful involvement. Whereas allowing something to die is a passive behavior even though it's still willful. Ideally, we want to kill the sin in our lives, but many times we've tried and failed. Or maybe we can't get up the courage to try. How can we help God's dying process, then, if we, by ourselves, can't kill this sin?

We can look back to the Old Testament for our answer. Old Testament folks couldn't kill their own sin any more than we can today; instead, they were commanded to sacrifice, to shed blood, to atone for their wrongdoing—the sins that were *killing* them. And in fact, the only way to heal from sin is to let something die or kill it. What can we sacrifice? Better yet, what are *ways* I can sacrifice? What is sacrificial behavior on my part? Prayer, fasting, tithing, spiritual disciplines, spending time reading the Bible when we want to watch TV, or being more relational when we want to be isolated are all examples of sacrifice. What's more, they're all possible for us, today, as a way to attack the sin in our life. It's interesting to note that the temple in Jerusalem was destroyed by the Roman Army in 70 CE.

As a result the Jewish culture stopped the practice of sacrifice. They stopped this practice because the last place allowed by God to sacrifice was the temple, and as a result of its destruction, the Jewish culture felt they had no proper place to offer them. The Torah specifically commands that sacrifices are only allowed to be offered in a place chosen by God.[6]

Sacrifice was very serious business! This is amazingly analogous to what Jesus has done through the crucifixion and ascension. We are now considered the temple of the Holy Spirit. Now we can sacrifice wherever we are and should attempt to put into practice ongoing sacrifices to the Lord. This will look different for every person.

We see sacrifice and spiritual disciplines throughout the Old Testament through the ways the Jewish people sanctified and consecrated themselves and their physical location in order to please God and experience His presence (without being killed—because sin dies in the presence of the Lord). Now, we do this within as a way to "kill" the sin or the vice that has captured our souls. This might be something we need to *do* or something we need to *stop doing*. It could be how I think, or how I manage my emotions. Am I practicing the love chapter? Loving my neighbor? This is where we specifically ask God what He wants. Some things may be obvious but, as you see in the Old Testament, the sacrifice rarely, if ever, looked like the sin it was dying for! If we let God be in control in any of these positive ways, He will follow through in helping with the tricky stuff—making our sin history.

God has a way for us to live. Without His plan in place, we are killing ourselves in small ways and big ways, but not always fatally; we are at the least killing our authentic selves. How are you killing yourself, taking matters into your own hands, fighting to keep the wrong things alive? What needs to die in your life that is not authentic to the real you, the authentic creation that God intended when He "knit you together in your mother's womb" (Psalm 139:13 NIV)? What died when Lazarus passed away, even though "Lazarus" did not die permanently? And when the thing that's killing you dies away, and your grave clothes are taken off, what will your new life look like? I'm excited to find out—are you?

Applicable scripture references for encouragement and reflection:

Romans 8:1–2 (NIV)
Life Through the Spirit
Therefore, there is now no condemnation for those who

are in Christ Jesus, because through Christ Jesus the law of the Spirit who gives life has set you free from the law of sin and death.

Romans 8:35-39 (MSG)

So, what do you think? With God on our side like this, how can we lose? If God didn't hesitate to put everything on the line for us, embracing our condition and exposing himself to the worst by sending his own Son, is there anything else he wouldn't gladly and freely do for us? And who would dare tangle with God by messing with one of God's chosen? Who would dare even to point a finger? The One who died for us—who was raised to life for us!—is in the presence of God at this very moment sticking up for us.

Do you think anyone is going to be able to drive a wedge between us and Christ's love for us? There is no way! Not trouble, not hard times, not hatred, not hunger, not homelessness, not bullying threats, not backstabbing, not even the worst sins listed in Scripture: They kill us in cold blood because they hate you. We're sitting ducks; they pick us off one by one. None of this fazes us because Jesus loves us. I'm absolutely convinced that nothing—nothing living or dead, angelic or demonic, today or tomorrow, high or low, thinkable or unthinkable—absolutely *nothing* can get between us and God's love because of the way that Jesus our Master has embraced us.

Galatians 2:20 (NIV)
I have been crucified with Christ and I no longer live, but Christ lives in me. The life I now live in the body, I live by faith in the Son of God, who loved me and gave himself for me.

Galatians 2:19-21 (MSG)
What actually took place is this: I tried keeping rules and working my head off to please God, and it didn't work. So I quit being a "law man" so that I could be God's man. Christ's life showed me how, and enabled me to do it. I identified myself completely with him. Indeed, I have been crucified with Christ. My ego is no longer central. It is no longer important that I appear righteous before you or have your good opinion, and I am no longer driven to impress God. Christ lives in me. The life you see me living is not "mine," but it is lived by faith in the Son of God, who loved me and gave himself for me. I am not going to go back on that. Is it not clear to you that to go back to that old rule-keeping, peer-pleasing religion would be an abandonment of everything personal and free in my relationship with God? I refuse to do that, to repudiate God's grace. If a

living relationship with God could come by rule keeping, then Christ died unnecessarily.

2 Corinthians 5:17 (NIV)

Therefore, if anyone is in Christ, the new creation has come: The old has gone, the new is here!

Isaiah 44:22 (NIV)

I have swept away your offenses like a cloud, your sins like the morning mist. Return to me, for I have redeemed you.

Isaiah 44:21–23 (MSG)

Remember these things, O Jacob. Take it seriously, Israel, that you're my servant. I made you, *shaped* you: You're my servant. O Israel, I'll never forget you. I've wiped the slate of all your wrongdoings. There's nothing left of your sins. Come back to me, come back. I've redeemed you." High heavens, sing! GOD has done it. Deep earth, shout! And you mountains, sing! A forest choir of oaks and pines and cedars! GOD has redeemed Jacob. GOD's glory is on display in Israel.

Lamentations 3:58 (NIV)

You, Lord, took up my case; you redeemed my life.

Matthew 9:36 (NIV)

When he saw the crowds, he had compassion on them, because they were harassed and helpless, like a sheep without a shepherd.

Reflection Questions:

1. Which of the above reflection verses spoke to your heart, which did you find hard to believe, and which of the verses do you need to believe? Pick some of the verses to memorize and speak to God about.

2. In reference to the passage in the twenty-first chapter of Numbers shared at the beginning of this chapter, are you willing to tell you God you are sorry for any character issues you may have and for accusing Him of "what *you* think His motives are for why you are where you are"? Are you willing to *look* at the thing that is killing you? What are your character issues that may require acknowledgement and repentance? Are you willing to look at the cross and believe that Christ's death and resurrection is the antidote for whatever it is that is killing you and keeping you from the abundant life?

3. From the story of Lazarus, what are you afraid is "permanent" versus trusting Jesus that it may only be "fatal"? Are you willing to say, "Thy will be done," and trust that God can heal and nourish the good thing He is working in you?

4. What character(s) do you most relate to in the Lazarus story, and why? What needs to change now that you have awareness/insight? What is God revealing to you about yourself and about Himself? Pick one or more of the characters and use the "Ignatian Way" to prayerfully meditate with God to discover what He wants to show you about yourself. You may be surprised when He shows you positive things as well as some changes you may need to face.

5. Are you able to apply the "love chapter" to your own life? Are you able to love yourself the way God loves you? Are you willing to practice the 2nd command of the New Testament: *And the second is like it: "Love your neighbor as yourself"* (Matthew 12:39 NIV)? If not, what is getting in your way? Is it something like condemnation, shame, refusing to forgive yourself, etc.?

6. What part of the scriptures moves you or touches your heart? What is God speaking to you through His word, and what verses does He want you to take to heart?

7. What has happened in your past that continues to be in your present and is affecting your future because it is unresolved? What is, unfortunately, still alive and active? What thing, event, hope, dream, mistake, lost opportunity, etc., continues to **separate** you from experiencing the "love of God" in Romans 8:38 and, so aptly expressed, in 1 Corinthians 13, the "love chapter"?

8. What is your understanding about legalism? Are you willing to embrace radical forgiveness, even radical acceptance? To learn more about how legalism may be infecting your relationship with your Creator, yourself, and others, see the book recommendations section (p. 198).

9. Consider Romans 6:7: "because anyone who has died, has been set free from sin" (NIV). Take some truly reflective time and ask yourself and your God, "What needs to die so that I may be free?"

10. Take a moment here to ask yourself what is still grieving you about your past or what doesn't want to die. What might be the next step you need to take, to accept, and to grieve?

11. This might be rough; bear with me. Make a list of your obvious struggles, dysfunctions, or vices you indulge in—the things you feel guilty about. This isn't so God can condemn you, or so you can condemn yourself; it's so that you can get them down on paper and then listen to what God really wants to say to you. The enemy wants to condemn, but God, who sees the same sin, wants to set you free. Remember that in the Old Testament the sacrifices didn't match the sins; bear in mind that, likewise, the sacrifice God wants from you may not match your sin or even look like it applies.

12. One of the most pleasing sacrifices to God is humility. In what areas do you need humility, and who, or what, do you need to humble yourself over? A helpful verse for meditation is Psalms 139:23–24: *Search me, God, and know my heart; test me and know my anxious thoughts. See if there is any offensive way in me, and lead me in the way everlasting* (NIV).

13. Consider this strange question: Do you really want to get better? Jesus asked people if they wanted to be healed before He healed them, and for good reason. He is asking if we want to get better because He can heal us, but we may not be ready to stay committed to a lifestyle that the healing might afford or demand. Sometimes getting "better" isn't easy; many people would rather win the lottery than learn good financial management, and yet most lottery winners are bankrupt within a couple of years. Ask yourself how committed you are to change in order to have the life you desire, the abundant life. Talk with God about how hard this is, how scary or painful it is to go through the dying process, and how scary, painful, or disappointing it will be if you don't go through the process. Either way, you can know that God *never* gives up, He *never* quits, and He *will* complete the good work He has begun in all of us (Philippians 1:6). For focus and meditation, consider John 5:6: *When Jesus saw him lying there and learned that he had been in this condition for a long time, He asked him, "Do you want to get well?"*(NIV). Are *you* really in earnest about getting well?

14. If you have done any recovery work, this is also an opportunity to identify "character defects," or those things that need to change, that only our Higher Power can. This is the wonderful inspiration of the Serenity Prayer that *I will change the things I can and accept the things I cannot.*

Chapter 4

THE LIFE YOU'RE SETTLING FOR

We've seen that death is a necessary part of life—a necessary part of *your* life in order to promote growth and abundance. And, in fact, death in our lives happens all the time. This happens through the changes we experience and initiate, relationships we let go for one reason or another, and habits we don't hold on to. This happens as well through actions we change because of circumstances or a desire to "better ourselves." With every type of death, then, the question becomes, **are the *right* things dying?**

Or are the *wrong* things dying: such as your hope, your faith, your love for God, your love for self, and your love for others? Are your dreams or your trust in God's promises dying? Is your childlike wonder of God being replaced with cynicism or skepticism? Is the trial or hardship you're enduring producing jadedness or bitterness? Is this refining process just making you weary and giving you only a desire to quit?

Ask yourself this question: What is dying in me so that Christ may live in and through me? If you can't think of an answer, the wrong things might be dying.

We have many positive examples from the Bible: What needed to die while Lazarus was in the grave? What needed to die when Jonah was in the belly of the whale? What needed to die while Paul was blinded? What needed to die while Peter, after he betrayed Jesus, waited for Christ's forgiveness? Each of these people was fundamentally changed through the type of death they experienced.

Let's take a closer look at Peter, and compare him with another close compatriot of Jesus, another man who betrayed Him. His name is Judas. Have you noticed that while there are many Peters, Pauls, Davids, Thomases, Solomons, and Abrahams in this world, it's rare to find a Judas? No one names their child Judas; do *you* know anyone named Judas? A uniting factor among these men is their sin and a past that is slaughtered by mistakes. We revere all but one and model our lives after their repentance and faith. We are inspired by God's faithfulness, kindness, forgiveness, and process in their lives. And then there's Judas. Judas even repented: *"Judas the one who betrayed him, realized that Jesus was doomed. Overcome with remorse, he gave back the thirty silver coins to the high priests, saying, "I've sinned. I've betrayed an innocent man"* (Matthew 27:3–4 MSG). He verbalized his sin, gave back the money, *but* was only filled with remorse. He didn't like the outcome; it wasn't the way he wanted it to be. As we look at his life, we see that instead of his character flaws, his inauthentic self, dying that night with the Lord, instead we see he took his own life. He repented in a way; he admitted he was wrong and was emotionally devastated by it, but he did not accept or allow redemption or heart change. He stopped the sin outwardly but did not change internally. He turned from his sin of selling the life of Jesus, but turned around and sold himself out through suicide. Yet even Judas was not beyond redemption; if he would have resisted suicide, he could have received the life of Christ regardless of his life of sin. Just as Judas was, even we are not beyond redemption.

Peter, after his betrayal, initially went back to his old life, "his way," his own man-made solution; but he later went on to live a testimony of faith and forgiveness that has healed and inspired millions. Likewise, Judas could have let his pride, greed, and control die in the days after he betrayed the Lord, and he could have lived in a redeemed state just as Peter did. Instead, his story is one of derision, tragedy, shame, and negative instruction—in other words, how *not* to be. It's never any different with suicide.

This spirit of suicide, very prolific in today's world, is Satan's ploy straight from the pit of hell. As a "solution," it's not creative, personal, or unique. Do not entertain this idea; rather, actively renounce it. In my years of experience as a psychotherapist, I've found that in general most people don't really want to die; they simply don't know how to live, and they feel they can't continue to live in the pain that they are in. But what they don't understand is that listening to Satan's lies in our life actually takes us on a far longer, more dangerous path—one that's not in our own best interest—always intimating that Satan's way is the softer, shorter, less painful route.

However, God's way, while thorough, is always the shortest and least painful path to a better life. He does not enjoy our trials and tribulations the way our enemy does, but He also does not intend for us to need to re-do or re-learn parts of a painful process. While His path for us might not be easy, it will take us safely to our destination. Suicide, on the other hand, does not end in glory as the crucified life does; rather, it is an over-simplified solution that produces incredibly complicated issues for those left behind. It is never the answer. Suicide kills us in the body without resolving the turbulence of the soul. It's a classic example of allowing the wrong thing to die.

Judas thought his only value was in his performance. And yet Jesus called him friend, knowing who He was dealing with. Jesus was neither blind nor ignorant. He **chose** Judas to be his disciple and friend; and He was not shocked or surprised by Judas' negative behaviors. In fact, Jesus offered Judas the greatest gift of all: walking, talking, living, learning, and being loved by God his Creator. In the same way, God is not shocked or surprised by your sin and character flaws, but He gladly offers you, and everyone else, the same gifts of grace and forgiveness He would've given Judas.

No, Judas didn't do anything to shock Jesus; he only shocked himself, and this turned out to be a very painful thing (have you ever shocked yourself? It's more than uncomfortable!). Judas couldn't get over himself; he couldn't get past what he'd done. He couldn't see a solution to the mess he had created, and he allowed himself to listen to Satan's lies and Satan's solution.

Judas was keeping alive, and nursing, the qualities that should have been dying: qualities like pride, ego, fear, and shame, while killing the person that should have been living. This is an extremely crucial concept regarding the need to die to sin. When scriptures refer to us being "dead," this does not mean the cessation of being, but rather a condition of separation and alienation from God.[7] "Living in sin," then, is referring to a type of "living death" because we are in a state of active opposition against God. When Adam sinned, He went against God and separated himself from the "Life-giver." While humans are not able to indefinitely sustain life, they are able to end life.

This is what Judas did: *he ended his life rather than asking for help in ending his sin.* He became his own judge, his own prosecutor, his own jury, and ultimately his own executioner. He left out the most important position when a defendant has been brought to court: the defender! This would have been Jesus, who is our defender to the great and Almighty God, the ultimate Judge. We deserve to be in court, we have broken the law, but God works through Jesus to offer redemption instead of death. It's always a double tragedy when life ends in the absence of redemption. Now is a good time to consider what needs to die in you so that Jesus may comfort and weep with you and your loved ones as you go through your own refining and dying process—just as He did with Lazarus, his family, and his friends.

We all might, at times, find ourselves tempted to *pull a Judas*: to listen to Satan's lies about our situation. But don't fool yourself for a second that Satan has your best interest in mind, or that he "understands." The enemy has no right to speak into your life unless you let him—he is not your Creator! He is your accuser. He condemns. And while his lies might be veiled in fact (that you have sinned), he spins a web of deception around it. Whereas God knows the truth behind your sin—your hurt, confusion, insecurity, past wounds, deception, and so on—Satan uses the truth to manipulate, lie, confuse, distort, pervert, and mislead God's people. God speaks the "truth" to set you free; Satan speaks "facts" to create bondage! You must discern between Satan's voice, your voice, and the voice of God. Satan will always reveal himself through the darkening of condemnation versus the increase of faith and hope that comes with the Lord's conviction.

Remember, when you reflect on your circumstances, that sin is common to mortal man, regardless of one's station in life, education, money, prestige, poverty, sickness, etc. Sin occurs at all levels of existence; and while you may have shocked and surprised yourself, that is not God's position. We often become desperate to get out of the circumstance we have created for ourselves. We seem to think we know a better, faster, shorter route out of our sin. God says to us in Proverbs 14:12: *There is a way that appears to be right, but in the end it leads to death* (NIV). This was Judas' downfall.

God's love, unlike ours at times, is not too shallow or weak to forgive and restore. Judas tried to be a god in his own life and tried to "fix" what he'd done by confessing: "I have sinned. I've taken the life of an innocent man." He even gives back the 30 pieces of silver. Although it was a confession, it was quite passive–aggressive and extremely immature (one of our defense mechanisms) because he knew the priests couldn't use "blood money" as an offering in the temple. He then takes his own life. You belong to God; He bought you with a high price and died so you don't have to. He wants to live with you regardless of your weaknesses and your failings. It bears repeating: His ways are not our ways; His thoughts are not our thoughts (Isaiah 55:8). It's about Judas that Christ was quoted as saying in Matthew 26:24: *"Woe to the man who betrays the Son of Man! It would be better for him if he had never been born"* (NIV). Christ didn't say this in disgust or anger; He said it with much love and pity. Could the real betrayal be Judas' refusal of his forgiveness, his redemption, and his life? While Peter's betrayal was soon forgiven and redeemed, Jesus would weep over Judas because Judas' chapter was over. His betrayal was not the shortest verse in his life; rather, it became the longest chapter because it was to be his last one, his eternal one. Don't let Christ weep because your own hands finished your chapter. Let him weep instead with compassion due to your suffering. He loves you, and He hates the pain you're in! Let him weep with you as he did with Mary and Martha. Let Him weep with you as

He walks with you the way of redemption, for you and your life.

> "For his anger lasts only a moment, but his favor lasts a lifetime; weeping may stay for the night, but rejoicing comes in the morning." (Psalm 30:5 NIV)

The Lord knew that joy, promise, and new life were coming through Lazarus' death and through Peter's dying process. His anger and sadness over death—both His own and the deaths that result from our deadly sins—only last for a moment, because He knows that rejoicing and promise are just around the corner, for eternity, to be lived out on earth and then in heaven. Do not be tempted to translate God's actions through your own shame, relational hardships, or failures. God is telling us who He is! He is telling us that He understands people and their pain, that His anger is short lived, and that He is *constantly* working for our success. Take heart, it's good news! Read the following verse, and consider how you can use its message in your life:

> A Message from the high and towering God, who lives in Eternity, whose name is Holy, "I live in the high and holy places, but also with the

low-spirited, the spirit-crushed, and what I do is put new spirit in them, get them up and on their feet again. For I'm not going to haul people into court endlessly, I'm not going to be angry forever. Otherwise, people would lose heart. These souls I created would tire out and give up. (Isaiah 57:15–17 MSG)

We all have a tendency to be like Judas. We all suffer from a pride that will not let us see any other way than our own solutions. In Judas' mind, and in his world, he had gone too far. He believed his behaviors were too low, too bad, too big for even God, but only because Judas saw through his eyes, not through God's. Take a look at God's perspective:

So, what do you think? With God on our side like this, how can we lose? If God didn't hesitate to put everything on the line for us, embracing our condition and exposing himself to the worst by sending his own Son, is there anything else he wouldn't gladly and freely do for us? And who would dare tangle with God by messing with one of God's chosen? Who would dare even to point a finger? The One who died for us—who was raised to life for us!—is in the presence of God at this very moment sticking up for us. Do you think anyone is going to be able to drive a wedge between us and Christ's love for us? There is no way! Not trouble, not hard times, not hatred, not hunger, not homelessness, not bullying threats, not backstabbing, not even the worst sins listed in Scripture: They kill us in cold blood because they hate you. We're sitting ducks; they pick us off one by one. None of this fazes us because Jesus loves us. I'm absolutely convinced that nothing—nothing living or dead, angelic or demonic, today or tomorrow, high or low, thinkable or unthinkable—absolutely nothing can get between us and God's love because of the way that Jesus our Master has embraced us. (Romans 8:31–39 MSG)

A Tale of Two Sons and Two Sins

But there are many more ways to errantly undergo the dying process, whether we ignore our problems, postpone our journey to abundance, deny the fact that we need change, or simply run away from God's calling—as did Jonah and another key fictional character from the New Testament, the prodigal son. The story, told by Jesus, is found in Luke 15:11–32 (MSG):

Then he said, "There was once a man who had two sons. The younger said to his father, 'Father, I want right now what's coming to me.' So the father divided the property between them. It wasn't long before the younger son packed his bags and left for a distant country. There, undisciplined and dissipated, he wasted everything he had. After he had gone through all his money, there was a bad famine all through that country and he began to hurt. He signed on with a citizen there who assigned him to his fields to slop the pigs. He was so hungry he would have eaten the corncobs in the pig slop, but no one would give him any. That brought him to his senses. He said, 'All those farmhands working for my father sit down to three meals a day, and here I am starving to death. I'm going back to my father. I'll say to him, Father, I've sinned against God, I've sinned before you; I don't deserve to be called your son. Take me on as a hired hand.' He got right up and went home to his father. When he was still a long way off, his father saw him. His heart pounding, he ran out, embraced him, and kissed him. The son started his speech: 'Father, I've sinned against God, I've sinned before you; I don't deserve to be called your son ever again.' But the father wasn't listening. He was calling to the servants, 'Quick. Bring a clean set of clothes and dress him. Put the family ring on his finger and sandals on his feet. Then get a grain-fed heifer and roast it. We're going to feast! We're going to have a wonderful time! My son is here—given up for dead and now alive! Given up for lost and now found!' And they began to have a wonderful time. All this time his older son was out in the field. When the day's work was done he came in. As he approached the house, he heard the music and dancing. Calling over one of the houseboys, he asked what was going on. He told him, 'Your brother came home. Your father has ordered a feast—barbecued beef!—because he has him home safe and sound.' The older brother stalked off in an angry sulk and refused to join in. His father came out and tried to talk to him, but he wouldn't listen. The son said, 'Look how many years I've stayed here serving you, never giving you one moment of grief, but have you ever thrown a party for me and my friends? Then this son of yours who has thrown away your money on whores shows up and you go all out with a feast!' His father said,

'Son, you don't understand. You're with me all the time, and everything that is mine is yours—but this is a wonderful time, and we had to celebrate. This brother of yours was dead, and he's alive! He was lost, and he's found!'"

Look again to these key portions:
- "When he came to his senses" (literally, this means "sober-mindedness, bottomed-out")
- "Father, I've sinned against God, I've sinned before you; I don't deserve to be called your son ever again."
- "Your brother came home. Your father has ordered a feast—barbecued beef!—because he has him home safe and sound."

Just like Lazarus did, the prodigal son needed to reach a place in which he died to a former life—literally bottomed out—so he could live a new, redeemed one. Lazarus required a physical death; the lost son, on the other hand, experienced different kinds of sicknesses: addictions, defiance, arrogance, and rebellion, to name a few. All humans are susceptible to these; perhaps you can think of some in your life (I can for mine). Jesus also died for the sin of self-will, the idea of "I will do it 'my way,'" I know what's best," and, "I don't need help; no one else 'gets it.'"

But the lost son himself isn't the only one with a dying process to face. His older brother, clearly, is at a crossroads. We do not know if he is willing to endure the work that needs to be done in his own life, and to take the path that God has laid in front of him, but we can see that he needs change or he will forever be stifled by his legalism. His outcome will be all-too-familiar with Job's wife.

Perhaps you can think of a situation in which you relate to either brother. So I now ask you the following questions:

1. Do you need to "come to your senses"?
2. Are you judging someone that has "come to his or her senses"?

If you identify with the second question, you might be thinking that this person still needs to face consequences for their actions—coming to their senses isn't enough. They need to pay somehow. This is our concept of "fairness." It's not "fair" that the other person simply gets away with all they've done. We should be rewarded for keeping the faith. But have you considered the fact that it's extraordinarily difficult to be on the same page as God when you're in this mindset? It's not uncommon to feel this way; you may even feel like this toward yourself. Consider that He's forgiven *everything* and is rejoicing over the one who was lost.

And now a third question: Will you realize that this person is God's problem and not yours? In the story of the prodigal son, we see only the homecoming celebration and the father's re-institution of his son into right standing as a full-fledged family member. God rejoices over us, too, when we return to Him. What we don't see is what happens after the celebration. I'm not suggesting that the father takes his wrath out on the son to the full extent of his rights and capabilities, but we also don't see any indication that there will be an absence of consequences. The son, after all, spent his entire inheritance, which likely won't be replaced. What's more, the father isn't naïve or foolish; he knows full well that although his son, thankfully, survived his sinful sojourn, it doesn't mean there's no "cleanup" to be done. If you've ever dealt with someone who's gone through this type of recovery, you may know the feeling. We're grateful they didn't die, but that doesn't change the fact that there's a lot of work in their future. We know that anyone with a past of this nature is plagued by residue and, until it is resolved, it's still following him or her. The prodigal son is no longer "killing himself" with his sin, but now he needs to know how to live!

The prodigal son is more than willing to do the

work it takes; he's experienced the alternative, a journey of "self-discovery" that has only brought him embarrassment, dishonor, and upset. What's more, he's showing true repentance in that he doesn't feel entitled to anything. He's simply hoping to labor and earn a few meals (not even the wealth he'd had before) and is astonished to instead find himself joyously welcomed back as a family member. This younger brother, who almost lost his life, now seems to understand Matthew 16:26: "What good will it be for someone to gain the whole world, yet forfeit their soul? Or what can anyone give in exchange for their soul?" (NIV). In their quest to attain the addictions of the world (fame, money, drugs, elusive "happiness," etc.), many lose things much more rare: family, friends, and their soul—their "real" personhood and original design.

On the other hand, we see the older brother's annoyance and, if we're honest, some of us may feel like we can see his point. But as the story points out, haven't we gotten our reward every day as we have lived and served our Father? We see that maybe the older brother's "good works" were not so much out of a servant's heart but were more pharisaical or performance-oriented. He might have been doing the right things for the wrong reasons; or possibly, like with Judas, the wrong things are dying. This brother will have to "bottom out" differently than the younger brother. We hope he can push aside his jealousy, join in the celebration, and reap the steady benefits of serving a gracious Father rather than head down the path of the sin of legalism.

We've now looked at a few examples of men who have died to the wrong things: Judas tried to escape through suicide while the prodigal son, at the outset of the story, denied his father and home and went his own way in sin (acting as if his father had died, and he has now gained his inheritance). But as we saw with the older brother in the story of the prodigal son, another way to die to the wrong thing is to miss entirely the message of what Jesus came to teach us. It goes to show that even by leading a "perfect" life, or attempting to, you're not free from the possibility of having died to the wrong thing. And, as a result, you may be actually living in sin. Legalism is a type of sin that affects a huge number of Christians to some degree. And while judging others is one thing, judging ourselves is yet another. Even if your past resembles the prodigal son's a little too closely for your own comfort, you're not called to be your own judge and jury.

> You have searched me, LORD, and you know me. You know when I sit and when I rise; you perceive my thoughts from afar. You discern my going out and my lying down; you are familiar

with all my ways. Before a word is on my tongue you, LORD, know it completely. You hem me in behind and before, and you lay your hand upon me. Such knowledge is too wonderful for me, too lofty for me to attain. Where can I go from your Spirit? Where can I flee from your presence? If I go up to the heavens, you are there; if I make my bed in the depths, you are there. If I rise on the wings of the dawn, if I settle on the far side of the sea, even there your hand will guide me, your right hand will hold me fast. If I say, "Surely the darkness will hide me and the light become night around me," even the darkness will not be dark to you; the night will shine like the day, for darkness is as light to you. (Psalm 139: 1–12 NIV)

Nothing you have done is so shameful that you're unlovable; nothing is so terrible that God can't use it for good. There's nothing you can't recover from; nothing is too big for God. He has a way: His way.

[18] "But forget all that— it is nothing compared to what I am going to do.[19] For I am about to do something new. See, I have already begun! Do you not see it? I will make a pathway through

the wilderness. I will create rivers in the dry wasteland. (Isaiah 43:18–19 NLT)

What's the Difference?

Peter betrayed Christ, returned briefly to his old life to try to figure things out, and finally ended up dying to this old life and living a new, better, and more abundant one. Judas gave in to lies, pride, and despair. The prodigal son tried to find happiness his own way and then returned to his father's abundant house. His older brother lived among the abundance but may never have died to his own legalism and enjoyed what he had. We see stories like these all the time. Peter's life and the prodigal son's life couldn't have been more different even after their return to God's "way," but the thing they had in common was marked abundance after they had undergone the dying process to former lives and their own self-will.

Which begs the question: What could your life look like if you weren't settling for a fishing boat, or a pig sty, or a strict adherence to legalism in your own life and the lives of others? What if you let the thing that's killing you die?

Reflection Questions:

1. When you read the statement: "Are the *right* things dying," how might you respond to it? In contrast, how might you respond to the statement: "Are the *wrong* things dying?" Are you allowing for more and more of your life to end, versus asking instead for help to end the sin? It is very important that we incorporate the following biblical passage into our lives:

   > ¹⁶ Confess to one another therefore your faults (your slips, your false steps, your offenses, your sins) and pray [also] for one another, that you may be healed *and* restored [to a spiritual tone of mind and heart]. The earnest (heartfelt, continued) prayer of a righteous man makes tremendous power available [dynamic in its working]. (James 5:16 AMP)

2. If you were to be honest, which of the biblical characters did you relate most with, and why? Would it be Peter, Judas, King David, Solomon, Jonah, Job, Job's wife, or Lot's wife? What other biblical characters fit for you, and why? What traits, thoughts, feelings, or behaviors

might you share with them? And what can you learn from their life stories?

3. What is your *old way*: the comfortable and/or familiar way you might go back to or stay in when things get hard, don't make sense, or seem hopeless?

4. Have you ever considered suicide or just wished it could somehow be over: *can I be done yet*? If so, what are you willing to ask God for again? The most tragic aspect of Judas' suicide was that God truly understood his shame, panic, tunnel vision, and desperation. God had a way for Judas even after all he had done, he still could have made a good thing out of the terrible thing he had done. Even if your thoughts of death are not due to some horrific mistake, please understand that suicide is the "biggest mistake" you'll ever make; it is not a mistake that can be forgotten or undone. Whereas I do not believe suicide leads to hell, I do know it is hellish for those left behind. Please understand: God has great compassion and tenderness toward anyone who struggles with this pain; He is not asking for you to believe He can change anything. He is

simply asking for time. Are you willing to give God time to make a way for you to live? Are you willing to give yourself time? If you have ever talked with anyone who has struggled with this feeling, you will not find someone that regrets living; you will only find a person that is thankful they waited.

5. Do you get over-focused on your performance and others' opinions of you? Meditate on the following "formula" which God gave me years ago as a way to re-focus myself on the truth versus the lies our culture and Satan wanted me to believe: God's opinion + Jesus' performance = my self-worth/value (versus trying to be perfect and manage what others thought and felt about me, which always resulted in feelings of failure and distress).

6. Do you know the difference between your voice, Satan's voice, and the voice of God in your life? Who is doing the talking, and whom are you listening to? Journaling helps this process immensely.

7. Do you need to "come to your senses" as the prodigal son did? Are you stubbornly pushing for "your way," or are you afraid to trust "God's way"? If you have repented, have you forgiven yourself as your heavenly Father has? Are you being your own judge, prosecutor, jury, and executioner or jailer?

8. Are you judging someone that has "come to their senses"? Are you judging someone that is still living a prodigal life or some parts of it? Are you frustrated or angry that they are not receiving the consequences they deserve? Are you being judge, prosecutor, jury, and jailer toward them?

9. Are you willing to let that person be "God's problem" subsequently praying for them and thanking God for His goodness in your life? Are you willing to let go of the "fairness doctrine" realizing that God is not being "fair" with you? We all deserve so much more consequence than we receive. I am very thankful that I don't "reap everything I sow." I practice being grateful for God's mercy and graciousness in my life.

10. What would your life look like if you were to let the things that are killing you die? Imagine what God's version of your future life will look like if you are willing to go through the dying process with Him? Conversely, what *will* your future look like if you don't?

Chapter 5

HOW DO I MAKE THE PAIN STOP?

Jesus wept.

The above statement is the thirty-fifth verse in the eleventh chapter of John. Although it is the shortest verse in the entire Bible, it is by far one of the most poignant and endearing moments in the life of Christ. These two words say so much, speak so much, and tell us so much on so many different levels.

In the previous chapter we looked deeply into the story of Lazarus, a beloved man who died. His dying process, and subsequent death, reveal tremendous grief, loss, bewilderment, anger, shock, uncertainty, and hurt—only to name a few of the feelings and thoughts experienced within this story. The loss of something we love, something we have become attached to, or something we have hoped for is such a familiar pain to all humans; although each of us experiences our own unique version of this pain.

The statement, "The only way out is through," very succinctly explains this problem of pain we all have. We would all love to go around the pain, over the pain, even under the pain, but *through* the pain? There must be a different way! We all know of people, and have read about different individuals, who did not successfully manage pain. You see, pain demands a response, regardless of the size or impetus. In previous chapters we have addressed the things that may cause pain, the need to manage pain, and the purpose(s) of pain. In this chapter we will work through "how" to deal with pain, heal from pain, and grow from the pain, so that the pain of loss will be "for our gain, and not in vain."

Why is the famous verse, "Jesus Wept," so powerful? The mere fact that, in a literary sense, the author has it stand alone tells us God wants to make a point. There is something here for us. Physically God understands the need for tears and the expression of them. Tear composition varies from tear types. Mainly, tears are composed of water, salts, antibodies and lysozymes (antibacterial enzymes). According to a discovery by Dr. William H. Frey II, a bio-chemist from St. Paul Ramsey Medical Center in Minnesota, the composition of tears caused by emotion differs from that of tears as a reaction to irritations, such as onion fumes, dust, or allergy. Emotional tears are composed of more protein-based hormones, such as prolactin, andrenocorticotropic, and leucine enkephalin (a natural pain killer); this is suggested to be the mechanism behind the experience of crying from emotion making an individual feel better.

Jesus needed to feel better, and this gave Him strength even though crying is so often characterized as "being weak." We see here a perfect example of Jesus being "fully human" and operating as a human in a most healthy way as well as responding appropriately to his friends and community. This emotional expression strengthened and helped Him do the work that needed to be done. Are you familiar with the Scripture references regarding the "weeping and wailing women"?

Jeremiah 9:17 (MSG)
A Life That Is All Outside but No Inside
[17-19] A Message from GOD-of-the-Angel-Armies:
"Look over the trouble we're in and call for
help.
    Send for some singers who can help us mourn
our loss.
Tell them to hurry—
    to help us express our loss and lament,
Help us get our tears flowing,
    make tearful music of our crying.
Listen to it!
    Listen to that torrent of tears out of Zion:
'We're a ruined people,
    we're a shamed people!
We've been driven from our homes
    and must leave our land!'"

Why would they come, and why would they be called forth? For one, the incident deserves it; it memorializes the significance! Secondly, it is necessary as a way to move forward; and thirdly, there is healing physically in crying over the loss. Have you experienced this phenomenon at funerals when you are moved by the pain of another? The first verse in this passage says, *Look over the trouble we're in and call for help. Send for some singers who can help us mourn our loss; tell them to hurry—to help us express our loss and lament; help us get our tears flowing.* God understands that this world hardens us, and we need help to "feel" the feelings appropriate to our situation. We need to know that the expression of pain is actually healing, and the need to be vulnerable and connected with others strengthens us individually and collectively. Don't you find the statement, "There's not use crying over spilt milk," interesting? It sounds very logical to our human mind, but it is exceedingly unhealthy when we understand how God has designed us. This statement, while it may "feel" better temporarily and protect us from feeling vulnerable in the midst of others, it ushers in a whole host of problems.

  Satan wants us to minimize our pain and maximize our pleasure as a way to thwart the process of achieving a full, rich, and abundant life. He is intent on impeding the process of the good work God has begun in us, the work that causes us to be the vest version God has destined us to be.

How to do it: Grief and Loss Process
Developed by Elisabeth Kübler-Ross

The five stage model of grief and loss was first introduced by Swiss-American Psychiatrist Elisabeth Kübler-Ross in her 1969 book, *On Death and Dying*, and was inspired by her work with terminally ill patients. [8] Though it applies to the idea of death and dying in the physical realm, we can apply this concept to the death and dying of our self-will. This process will allow us to use our free will to choose God's will for our lives. The five stages, listed below, will be covered in more depth later in this chapter:

> **Stage One:** Shock and Denial
> **Stage Two:** Bargaining
> **Stage Three:** Anger
> **Stage Four:** Sadness and Mourning
> **Stage Five:** Acceptance

As always, there can be impediments to our healing process as we move through the five stages. We employ these often without even being consciously aware of their derivation or impact. These maladaptive coping skills are employed as a way of avoiding or ignoring going through the difficult process of grief and effectively healing from our pain:

Denial

Avoidance

Withdrawal/Isolation

Addictions/Compulsive Behaviors

Aggression

Control Issues

Emotional Shutdown/Numbing

Resistance

Rationalization

Minimizing

Dissociation

Intellectualizing

Projection

Displacement

Manipulation

I will be the first to admit that though the grief/loss process is effective, it is most certainly not pleasant. The maladaptive coping skills listed above are common to all human experience. We must remember, however, that it is God's healing plan for us to travel through each step, recognizing that He can and will use the changes that are uncovered through the process to produce our own abundant life. The grief and loss process gives opportunity for God to remove things in order to create space for the better thing(s) in your life. Let's take a look at each of these maladaptive coping skills individually and discover the ways in which they sabotage the healing process of grief and loss. These are oftentimes referred to as defense mechanisms, but we will be referring to them most often as maladaptive coping skills as our primary focus is addressing emotional pain and growth rather than the protection of the ego. While this is a fairly exhaustive list, it is not complete; however, it provides helpful focus and direction.

Denial: One of the "majors" and therefore quite predominant. Ignoring and/or refusing to acknowledge a behavior or part of the self is what characterizes this maladaptive coping skill. This is seen quite frequently in individuals and family systems needing to face an addiction issue. Or the individual may be denying a financial problem, health issue, or relationship problem, etc. This is also seen within the "grief and loss process" as a resistance to believe or "take in" that an extremely painful event or tragedy has occurred, or is occurring.

Avoidance: Is a maladaptive coping skill that is

characterized by a pervasive pattern of avoiding or withdrawing from social interaction, unpleasant situations, or anything that has to do with the painful event. The person will avoid people, places, conversations, and activities that remind him of his pain or create some measure of pain: "I don't want to bring it up and make it worse," or, "There's no point in talking about it; it's already done. Let's not re-hash it." For example, one might not answer their phone on a consistent basis because of the anxiety they feel regarding the unknown, or what might be expected of them.

Withdrawal/Isolation: This is a more severe form of defense. It entails removing oneself from events, stimuli, interactions, etc. under the fear of being reminded of painful thoughts and feelings. We feel that if we can "remove ourselves" from the event (or our life), we can protect ourselves from the pain we are feeling. We might try to "numb" our emotions, deny them, or stuff them in order to protect ourselves from the pain we are feeling. This might look like resisting invitations that one normally accepted or refusing to participate in normal life events (such as refusing to go to church or family get-togethers). People can also withdraw emotionally and still be present physically. When this defense mechanism is present, it may be a sign of underlying clinical depression.

Substance Addictions and/or Compulsive Addictions: In my experience I have become aware of two types of addictive behaviors. The first one being most obvious—that is, an addiction to some type of substance that our body would otherwise live without. For example, alcohol, tobacco, street drugs, narcotics, etc. This type of addiction is introduced to the body and is used frequently enough that the body experiences great distress, and possible death, if the substance is withheld. The second category is made up of compulsive behaviors. For example, eating disorders, sex and gambling addictions, shopping, hoarding, perfectionism, or even religion, to name a few. Both categories hold our mind, soul, and spirit hostage. The initial need for the addiction is generally pain-related. The problem is that the pain of addiction always becomes greater than the original pain.

Aggression: This defense mechanism is a way to deflect from thinking about or feeling whatever is the source of anxiety. Generally the anxiety is something that is out of the person's control, and/or it could be an event that provokes the less-empowering feelings such as, but not limited to, vulnerability, hurt, sadness, and/or fear. Aggression becomes a way to protect oneself. Aggressive people are usually anxious about something and trying to avoid the emotion involved with the anxiety. The focus is on the external world (people, places, and things) as a way to resist or avoid dealing with the emotions in their internal world. This defense mechanism is usually tangled up with control and manipulation. This is due to the degree of fear that it provokes in others who are experiencing the aggressive behaviors or attitudes. The aggressive behaviors may be physical (yelling, throwing things, shoving, name-calling, hitting, etc.). Or they may be more emotional in nature such as, bullying, intimidation, exhortation, or blackmail to get what the individual needs or wants.

For example, one sibling may tell another sibling that he/she will expose a secret unless he/she is allowed financial control over the parents' estate. A more subtle form of aggression is the passive version of it; this is more covert than overt. Passive-aggressive behavior is a form of covert abuse. If someone yells at you, throws things, or hits you, you "know" that you are being abused; it is *overt*. It is obvious and easily identified. Covert abuse is subtle, veiled, or disguised by actions that may even appear normal, and may even "seem" loving and caring. Oftentimes others can't "see" this type of aggression; however, the individual the behaviors are directed at "feels" it. Because of its covert nature it is very difficult to confront. This is due in part to the subconscious nature of passive-aggression; sometimes the individual has not, or cannot, admit to themselves the fact of their own anger: this is also known as "displaced anger." Some examples of this are procrastination, chronic lateness, obstructionism, "forgetfulness," "white lies," blame-shifting, withholding, sarcasm, and to name a few.

Control Issues: When someone is in terrible grief, they might try to control what they can—including the little things that really shouldn't matter. This becomes unhealthy if the need to control doesn't abate, and it could show up in controlling outcomes, rituals, micro-management, repressing feelings, or even using other defense mechanisms (aggression, resistance, deflection, shutting down, etc.) to feel in control as a way to avoid pain. These can include using manipulation as a way to control others' decisions, time, opinions, and so on and so forth.

Emotional Shutdown/Numbing/Repression: We pretend the feeling doesn't exist; this is different than "denying" a problem. When we deny, we ignore the problem; when we repress, numb ourselves, or emotionally shutdown, we are unable to access the feelings appropriate to the situation. We don't have healthy coping skills for emotion management, and so we "stuff," "forget," deny, deflect, or ignore the feeling.

Resistance: Resistance is often a form of deflection, similar to avoidance in some ways, and certainly a control issue. It might look like refusing to plan a funeral. Friends and family may see a lot of procrastination or micro-managing to the point that it is impossible to get the plan off the ground. Oftentimes we may feel "resistant" and not know why. For example, "I just don't want to read my Bible," or "I just don't want to go to such-and-such place, but I don't know why." This maladaptive coping skill is simply the resistance of some degree of discomfort and/or anticipated or projected pain. This can even occur in positive situations; for instance, a person is excited to be engaged, but can't seem to set a wedding date. The question to ask oneself is, "What is the resistance telling me; what's *under* my resistance; what might I be attempting to avoid by resisting?"

Rationalization (making excuses): This mechanism describes a person using faulty and false reasoning to convince him or herself that no wrong was done and that everything's fine. It involves the use of other manipulative tactics such as minimization, justification, blame shifting, or the creation of "convenient excuses" to effectively explain away bad behavior.

Minimizing: A technique used when complete

denial or repression is implausible. It is a way to make painful, frightening, sickening situations more bearable. "If I can't avoid, deny, or ignore the issue or situation, I will make it less significant. I will minimize the effects and/or outcomes. This is often seen in abusive and manipulative people who wish to downplay their behaviors and maltreatment of others.

Dissociation: This defense mechanism can range from a mild detachment from immediate surroundings to more severe detachment from physical and emotional reality. In mild cases, dissociation seeks to minimize or tolerate stress—including boredom or conflict. It might show up as daydreaming while driving a vehicle. In more extreme cases, it can mean an altered state of consciousness. Some people refer to this as an "out-of-body experience," as though they are watching themselves. They might say, "I feel like I am in a movie, or in a dream." They may find it hard to connect with the world they're in or with the people they are around. It is a psychological defense that allows the person to distance themselves or avoid emotional distress by disconnecting psychologically while still being present.

Intellectualizing: This is a form of isolation in which the person focuses on the intellectual components of a situation so as to create distance from the associated anxiety-provoking emotions. The person tends to separate emotion from ideas, and to avoid unacceptable emotions by focusing on the intellectual aspects. The individual gets "lost in their head," thereby avoiding feelings and any emotional connection to others.

Displacement: This defense mechanism shifts sexual or aggressive impulses to a more acceptable or less-threatening target, redirecting emotion to a safer outlet. The attempt to separate the emotion from its real object and redirect the intensity of the feeling to someone or something that is less offensive or threatening helps the individual avoid dealing directly with what is frightening or threatening. For example, a mother may yell at her child because she is angry with her husband. Or a person may be afraid to confront their boyfriend or girlfriend regarding their behavior or rejection, so they will "take it out" on their friend who is safe and will forgive them.

Projection: Rather than acknowledge an unpleasant or "sick" part of yourself, you disown it or attribute to other people or situations. For example, you may accuse or assume others of the very characteristics present within yourself. "Blame shifting" and/or "deflection" can also characterize this negative coping skill. This phenomenon occurs in both positive and negative ways. If I struggle with dishonesty, I may struggle with trusting the motives of others. If I am more altruistic and forgiving, I may assume others are the same to the point of denial that there is evil in this world. By criticizing others, I may be externalizing the very trait that belongs to me. The things that bother me the most may be the things that most need to change in me.

Manipulation: The need to change the perception, opinions, or behaviors of others, many times through deceptive, exploitive, devious, and even abusive methods. This is an attempt to control the external world so as to reduce the pain, fear, anxiety, and cognitive/emotional dissonance within the individual's emotional world. We all manipulate variables throughout the day to get our needs met. The measure of dysfunction is directly related to the degree to which we "lose our self and gain the world" and/or the degree to which we will tolerate another's loss for our gain. Manipulation uses, and is bolstered by and supported with, many of the above maladaptive coping skills.

Although the list is lengthy, it is not a full explanation of the complicated intra-psychic processes that humans develop to manage and cope with their world, nor is it a scholastic endeavor to educate you on psychological phenomena of the human condition. This is rather a way to examine behaviors "safely" (without condemnation), realizing that the defense mechanisms, or maladaptive coping skills, were created by a deeper part of ourselves in order to protect us from harm. This is why in Psalms 51:5–6 the psalmist so aptly and eloquently speaks of our condition when he says: *"I've been out of step with you for a long time, in the wrong since I was born. What you are after is truth from the inside out. Enter me, then; conceive a new, true life* (MSG). We can rest and realize that God understands the human condition and that we **are** doing the "best we can." Truly, we know these behaviors aren't working for us; they increase our pain and loneliness. So I say to you, as I have come to say to myself, "Of course we are doing the best we can, why wouldn't we?" We use the negative coping skills to reduce anxiety, soften failure, lessen guilt, reduce cognitive dissonance, and increase feeling of self-esteem. I wish it worked! Sadly, all that is really accomplished through the use of these coping skills is a distorted reality, increased self-deception, and our becoming increasingly more fragile and maladaptive.

In fact, it's not even logical to think that I could do better. Why? Because doing "better" would, of course, decrease the pain and stress I'm feeling. And remember: it's in our nature to gravitate *away* from pain (hence the defense mechanism). Why would I "consciously" (the operative word) choose to do immoral or painful things that I might not be proud of? That makes no sense! So we realize that there is some faulty hard wiring in us, a default or automatic "help" response in our minds. This hard wiring (including use of the defense mechanisms listed above) may not actually be so helpful.

Think about it: if you really could do better on your own, you probably would have no need to *read* this book; furthermore, if "I" could do it on my own, I would have had no need to *write* this book.

I'm sure there is a group of people who enjoy their "fallen-ness" and do not see it as such; they are usually called "fools." Again, in making my case of desiring wholeness and healing, they would have never spent money on such a book as this. And if they inadvertently purchased it or it was given to them, they would not have made it through the first chapter. You see, we are all struggling.

And I know when you read this you are probably thinking, "No, Cinthia, I am not doing my best. I should be doing better. I must not be trying hard enough." Am I right? I was there, and I can easily still be there if I don't resist it. So I say to you, "Well if you can do better, then what's stopping you?" Then just DO it! If you "feel" like you can but haven't seemed to be able to overcome or let go through all your strivings, then maybe it's time to accept your limitations, not to be confused with "accepting our limitations as a way of life" but trusting

God's abilities and desire to bring wholeness and healing.

So we *do* accept defeat, huh? We accept our "can't" and trust God's "I Can"! We then discover, with God's illumination through the Holy Spirit, what we truly *can* do and then what we *should* do. I am now no longer in condemnation (with all its *shoulds* and *coulds* and *woulds*). I am working with my Creator on what my part is in the change process and in my own dying process, and I will do it with all my might to the glory of the God who saves!

What I have come to understand through my own stumbling and struggling is that I really *can't* do better when it comes to changing my own human hard wiring. I didn't create me. Many times I confound myself, and I don't even understand my own creation. I continue to learn and discover, through relationship with God, "who I am" and "how I am made." He understands me and understands that the hard-wiring of me is infected with a virus called sin. This *does not* ever excuse or condone the sin that these many defense mechanisms may bring or my fallen nature that continuously gravitates toward sin.

What the Lord has taught me about defense mechanisms is that I am to be compassionate with myself and with others and to realize that these occurred automatically and mostly without our knowing it. Initially, this was not a conscious choice, but it is one I am fully responsible for now. Furthermore, I *was* "my best version" at that time. However, God wants "His best version" of me in my life. He wants to do a new thing, if I will allow it. What might be present in my life that may "get in the way" of God doing the new thing in my life:

1. The lack of positive coping skills
2. The inability to manage stress well
3. A tendency to rely on defense mechanisms
4. Resisting the "Grief and Loss Process"
5. A general fear of pain itself

The defense mechanisms previously listed are examples of what humans may turn to when they don't effectively work through the grief and loss process in order to deal with the changes, hurts, losses, and necessary character development and growth in their lives. The goal, however, is to effectively manage the change and resultant stress. The grief and loss process was originally put forth by a woman named Elisabeth Kübler-Ross. It's important to understand that this was never intended to be characterized as a rigid process: it's a cycle. You may veer away from it a bit, experience it in a different order, and skip a stage (especially if the loss was a relatively minor one). In a significant loss, many of the stages may be revisited, many times, before you ultimately experience acceptance and forgiveness. Essentially, the five stages are not linear, and they are not equal in their experience. Each loss you incur within your day-to-day living and overall life is unique to you. It was best said by Elizabeth Kübler-Ross: "People's grief, and other reactions to emotional trauma, is as individual as a fingerprint."

Please realize: this grief and loss process happens in the smallest situations as well as the largest events. For example, if I miss the green light and have to wait for three minutes, I will quickly go through the process and "get over the loss of time" on the way to my destination. This, however, pales in comparison to the sudden loss of a loved one, or a woman who was date raped and may have lost her virginity, or the person in sales who has been working a deal for the last year only to have it stolen by a competitor through favoritism or nepotism.

The latter descriptions of loss may take two to five years to effectively "get over." In fact, I'm not sure we ever "get over" the loss of a loved one, the loss of a baby or child of any age, or a loss of a beloved friend. We can, however, "get on" and have a life that our loved one would be proud of and rejoice over as we move through the following healthy healing process. It's the healthy process toward acceptance and forgiveness that we should all be aiming for.

As you read the descriptors of each stage, think of a minor or major loss you've recently experienced. Perhaps something as minor as having your heart set on a favorite meal, but being told that the restaurant just ran out. You might think, "Oh, great. Now I have to settle for another dish." Or maybe your child just left for college, and you're not sure what to do with yourself. It might be that you've been doing so well in your recovery when you relapsed, and now you feel that you have to tell someone that you'd been doing so well, but are now ashamed and feeling badly about yourself. Or maybe you found someone you thought was the person for you (finally), and he/she told you last night that it's just not working, and they just don't feel it. Or perhaps you just watched a parent or child pass away last night, or you just received the news that someone close was killed in a car accident. You lost a sale, you missed a sale, you gained weight, you didn't get pregnant, you lost a job, or you lost a dream.

Now you fill in the blanks of what your loss is. It could be personal (about you) and reveal that you are not where you want to be. It could be a minor mishap/infraction with a significant relationship, or it may be a major loss or stress that feels completely unmanageable and impossible to face. Following are the stages of grief and loss. By focusing on this list, we can learn how to resist the unhealthy defense mechanisms and move effectively toward accepting something that we were not consulted on or asked out opinion about. It *happened*, and now we must deal with it. Even if we did it to ourselves, we still need to accept and/or forgive.

This is also understood as a "cycle." This is very important to understand as Dr. Kübler-Ross never intended for this to be characterized as a rigid process. Although it has all the characteristics of a process, a process is usually defined as uniformly-timed steps done in a rigid sequential series. As a result, we want to look at it as a model or framework that includes necessary elements within a process. You see, a model is better defined as a shape or a guide. It's important to realize that, within this process, you will most likely "veer" away from it and may not experience all of the five stages. Also, many of the stages may be revisited before you ultimately experience acceptance and/or forgiveness. (This is usually determinant on the size of the loss, i.e. missing the light versus the loss of a loved one, or the death of a dream).

Furthermore, the order of the process will most likely not always fit the order it is presented in. You may experience "ebb and flow" between the stages, in that it may be more transitory than progressive. This is to say the five stages are not linear; furthermore, they are not equal in their experience. Each loss you incur within your day-to-day living and overall life is unique to you. You may not have anger regarding loss where another may be "stuck" in anger.

Stages of the Grief and Loss Process

Shock: The initial reaction to loss is that of shock. It is the person's emotional protection from overwhelm; it's the mind refusing to "take in" the knowledge of the loss and what it may mean. It is an attempt to "slow down" the process, blunting the initial blow of overwhelm. What the person's mind knows to be true is impossible to believe. This is generally experienced as, "No, no, no! This can't be! I don't believe it!" In a major loss, it may end up with the individual fainting, collapsing, walking away, or going to sleep (these responses are usually exhibited when the event is "larger than life," e.g., the death of someone or any event proportionate in nature).

Denial: This is a conscious or unconscious refusal to accept facts, information, reality, etc. in direct relation to the situation. It can be considered a defense mechanism, but is in no way *initially* harmful or sinful; on the contrary, it is actually perfectly natural and helpful, as long as it is "a stage," and the person does not remain in denial. If the traumatic event can be ignored, some people may become locked in this stage (at which point denial becomes unhealthy) This often appears in relationships where one wishes to deny the level of dysfunction and/or abuse that may be occurring, e.g. the person with an addiction, the child that is being molested, the money that is being squandered, a dependent spouse who has no idea about the finances, or the unfaithful spouse, to name a few. However, more serious losses, such as death and endings, are far more difficult to deny. Another example could be a divorce. It did happen, the spouse is gone, the paperwork has been signed. However, denial can still be found in the form of, "I just can't believe it!" or "How could that have happened?" This oftentimes moves into bargaining.

> *Our "past" is always in our present, affecting and altering our future.*

Bargaining: Let's use the above example of denial of a divorce. We might see a tendency toward obsessive and ruminative thinking that sounds something like this: "If only I would have, should have, could have; if only (fill in the blank), then it would not have happened. It's the rehashing of how it happened, why it happened, or why it should have never happened. Think about the loss of a child, the loss of a job, or a significant relationship and the struggle to even come close to acceptance. There is a compulsion to go over the event in one's mind and hash it out with whoever will listen. The self-recrimination continues as to why it should have never happened, what could have been done, or should have been done.

Even the loss of something valuable, like a piece of jewelry for instance, causes us to be in some denial. "It's here somewhere; we'll find it." "I can't believe it, I should have been more careful!" Sound familiar? I have found (in my experience) that the bargaining stage is very popular for cultures that are very performance-oriented and adhere strongly to self-empowerment philosophies. You might hear someone in these cultures profess, "If I can think it, I can be it," "I can be whatever I want to be," and, "The only obstacle is me." This is especially predominant in the American culture, where we commonly feel that "if we can conceive it, we can achieve it." As a result, we have a very difficult time accepting something that we do not want to accept. We fall into the "coulda, woulda, shoulda, and if only" ways of thinking, to the degree that we are often trapped in these imaginations for a lifetime. We never come to terms with the loss and are always thinking it "didn't have to be." This leads to a perpetual feeling of loss, supported by depression and anger, which means our "past" is always in our present affecting and altering our future. Traditionally, the bargaining stage for people facing death (of themselves or another) involves attempting to bargain with God as to the outcome. "If I go to church from now on," "If I give up such and such," or "I will never do that again if," or "I will (fill in the blank); just don't let this happen or let it be true!"

People facing traumas not resulting in mortal death may bargain or seek to negotiate a compromise with the other person or company involved. For example, "Can we still be friends?" when facing a break-up or "Can you waive the late payment fee just this once?" when late on a bill. Bargaining rarely provides a sustainable solution, and people can become "stuck" within bargaining depending on the size or the viability of the loss.

However, an impending loss may benefit from bargaining; we see this so adroitly managed when Abraham was bargaining with God over the loss of Sodom and Gomorrah for his nephew, Lot, and his family in Genesis 18:16–33. Many times in therapy, relationships are saved because of an impending loss. Behaviors are changed to avoid the impending loss. However, "stuck-ness" occurs when I have bargained, the loss occurs, and I still emotionally/intellectually continue to rehash "what might have been." I am now lost in time, others have moved on, and I am stuck rehashing what "coulda, shoulda, woulda been if only...then." It is arrogance to refuse acceptance when the origins of the resistance are *selfishness* (I just want what I want; even if it is the death of a person, it becomes all about what is best for me), *pride* (it now makes me look bad), *greed* (I am entitled to good health, a certain amount of financial security, the affection of another, or the acclaim for my talents), *offense* (how dare this happen to me, how dare you do this to me), or the *refusal of God's sovereignty* (not your way, God, but MY way). We never think we sound this way inside until we have to face the grief and loss process; then we are many times (not all the time) astounded by our own arrogance, pride, or lack of faith.

Anger: The feeling of anger is such a normal part of experiencing loss. How could we not be angry over the fact that we have lost something valuable—a house, a deal, a person? Maybe we have lost our reputation or a dream. Of course, we should be angry. We need never apologize for the feeling of anger—after all, we read that God has experienced plenty of anger—although we may need to apologize and make amends for how we expressed it and/or how it manifested in our life. Think about how much anger and anguish God felt over the tremendous "loss" of innocence His children experienced after eating the forbidden fruit. He was angry over the consequence that was necessary and all that it entailed—ultimately, His son dying on the cross to undo Adam's choice.

Anger can manifest in different ways. People dealing with emotional upset may be angry with themselves, and/or with others, especially those close to them. They may not realize or comprehend the level of anger they are feeling or what they are even angry about. Furthermore, they may feel guilty about being angry. One of the defense mechanisms may be displacement and the anger coming out "sideways" or denying, rationalizing, or minimizing anger. For instance, imagine the anger you might feel if someone you love commits suicide. You may be sympathetic and understanding, even connected to the anguish they felt, but . . . killing themselves? That's a whole different level, and it's difficult, to say the least. How can you forgive them for that and for all the pain they left behind? Knowing that anger is expected and normal helps us stay detached (please note that "detachment" is different than "withdrawal") and non-judgmental when experiencing both our own anger and the anger of another who is experiencing loss.

Mourning/Sadness: When we enter this stage,

it usually indicates that we have begun to accept the reality of the loss and the actuality that it has truly occurred. It doesn't mean that we won't cycle back through some denial, anger, or bargaining, but we are now "landing" in the reality that the loss truly occurred and reversal is unlikely. The stage of "sadness and grief" oftentimes follows bargaining and anger because those stages are very tiring, and we eventually succumb to accepting (even if only for a moment) the reality of the loss. We are just too tired to be mad and too tired to bargain. Out of all the feeling realms (those being glad, sad, mad, and scared), sadness and mourning are the least energetic. This is one of the reasons why we may "get stuck" or "prefer" anger and bargaining (these stages are more action-oriented and cause us to not feel so helpless or resigned to the loss) versus the willingness to finally grieve the loss and feel sad. This is a very important step toward acceptance, and we may vacillate between bargaining, anger, sadness and mourning before we are ever able to completely grieve the loss and eventually accept the "new normal." However, please don't confuse depression and mourning.

Oftentimes an individual can become depressed due to the anger they are feeling, the inability or resistance to accept, and/or the exhaustion felt from anger and bargaining, as well as the possibility of a predisposed tendency toward clinical depression. These limited examples are different from what we see in the actual grieving process, and it's important to distinguish between the two—a job that's best left to a professional. Don't get me wrong, the above list can be precursors to the actual grieving/mourning process. What we see in the Old Testament is that there is a "time to mourn" (Ecclesiastes 3:4). The Jewish culture gives 30-40 days where there is no work done, and the mirrors are covered with black cloth. In the Old Testament, they would send out the "weeping and wailing women" as a way to help individuals access their ability to cry and as a precursor to the funeral procession. What we realize about the power and health of funerals is that they help people access tears that they would not otherwise be able to feel; this occurs many times when others are crying, as in hiring the "weeping and wailing women" as the Old Testament practice espouses. Of course this does not work for everyone. Some of us "shut down" when others feel feelings, and we are only able to access feelings when we are by ourselves. Either way, the feelings need to be felt. The distinction needs to be made as to whether or not it has become, or has exacerbated, a clinical depressive state. This determination is best left to a professional. It's natural to feel sadness and regret, fear, uncertainty, etc. It shows that the person has at least begun to accept the reality of the loss. I don't know about you, but I have had some major losses in my life, that were not about a person, but that I believe deserved a funeral. I felt like a funeral might have helped.

I Walked a Mile with Pleasure

I walked a mile with Pleasure;
She chatted all the way;
But left me none the wiser
For all she had to say.

I walked a mile with Sorrow,
And ne'er a word said she;
But, oh! The things I learned from her,
When sorrow walked with me.

- Robert Browning Hamilton [9]

Acceptance/Forgiveness: Again this stage definitely varies according to the person's situation, although it is broadly an indication that there is some emotional detachment and objectivity. People dying can enter this stage a long time before the people they leave behind, who must necessarily pass through their own individual stages of dealing with the grief. It is characterized by the ability to "move on" and the feeling of peace through forgiveness. There may still be transient feelings, but they are no longer consuming, debilitating, and in the "forefront" of the mind. The feelings or experience still contain energy/emotion, but may be vague, diffuse, on the outskirts, and more a "memory" than a current experience.

    This can be painful as well, which is why people oftentimes resist acceptance because the emotions may be the only thing left of the loss. For example, if I don't feel sad and miss the person, place, or thing, then there is nothing. At least I still have my sadness. If it is the death of a dream, acceptance can feel like acquiescence of a life goal, so now I have no vision, so I don't care, and apathy may set in. Acceptance always means "more reality" that death has really happened, and it is over.

    Maybe someone has been in denial to the fact that they will not have a child; but the woman is now entering menopause and, for the first time, it is really true. A child will not be conceived by her. It is now no longer deniable; it is not going to happen. It is the loss of a dream. Or the athlete who is now past the age of eligibility. There is now the heaviness of reality, coupled with freedom that he/she must move on and ask the Lord for a new vision. It really isn't going to happen. Maybe your kids are "launching" but not in the way you envisioned it. Maybe you are divorcing after 40 years of marriage, and you are finally willing to accept a life without that mate. All that time, and it didn't work? Maybe you need to leave a church that had otherwise seemed perfect, but you now no longer feel like it fits, and you are finally willing to leave.

Acceptance is both a passive and active state. It is the landing and leaving, the giving into or accepting of reality, while at the same time being willing to move. It's the big okay, the "it is what it is," and the feeling that not only do I have no fight left in me, but I no longer wish to fight the inevitable.

Forgiveness is oftentimes a part of acceptance because we have to forgive whomever, or whatever, created or supported the loss. Oftentimes it is a person.

> **Roadblocks to Effectively Managing Pain:**
> - The person may not recognize the change that has taken place (for example, an elderly parent can't drive anymore).
> - The person may not accept that the loss has occurred (for example, refusing to believe they are broken up).
> - The individual may not expect to mourn a loss other than from death.
> - Feelings such as anger, rejection, or guilt may complicate and obscure the underlying grief.
> - Loss may come from a socially stigmatized event—a suicide, a racial incident, an abortion, drug/alcohol problems, so a sense of shame may cause the person to avoid drawing attention to the pain.
> - Friends and family in a person's life may communicate discomfort or disapproval of any expression of pain.
> - The individual may have emotional blocks as a result of previous losses that have not been resolved and may be afraid to explore feelings related to a new loss.
> - A desire not to upset or add to the grief of others involved may cause a person to repress feelings.
> - Over-dependence on the lost person, place, or thing as a means of self-fulfillment or self-identity makes it hard to let go.
> - Hanging on to grief as a means of hanging on to that which was lost can keep a person from resolution of the loss: "the only thing I have left of the person/idea/place is my sadness or anger."
> - Sex-role or cultural conditioning can block the expression of feelings. For instance, what is an appropriate way for a man to feel and what is an acceptable way for a woman to feel loss, grief, and/or anger?

They betrayed us, they rejected us, they thwarted our success, they stole from us, or they abused us. Sometimes it is our body. We feel as if our body betrayed us, or let us down, or worked against us. Other times, it may be ourselves. We messed it up, we failed, or we got in the way of the good thing that was supposed to happen. And, sometimes, it is God. It seems strange to have to forgive God. I have had many talks with my patients, as well as myself, about the concept that I "hurt my feelings on God." I know that God is perfect and had my best interests in mind (the proverbial Jeremiah 29:11–13), but it sure didn't feel like that.

I have had to forgive God because my feelings got hurt, not because He did the wrong thing. He didn't do it my way, and I am now despondent. I have told patients several times, "You've had to forgive me; even though I did the right thing therapeutically, it still hurt your feelings." You see, bereavement is "what" I have lost, and grief is "how" I feel about it or my reaction to it. Grief is either something tangible, as in what I can touch or measure (a person, a job), or it can also be an abstract of what I expected, what I thought should be, what I dreamed would be, the way "life was supposed to go." This means that "the death of a good thing, for the better," and the "death of the thing that is killing me" will both experience acceptance, but it is possible that you may not need to work through forgiveness.

Note that even though this process is effective, it's not much fun—we may even see these steps as negative. Nevertheless, it's well within your humanity and God's healing plan for you to travel through each step, recognizing that God can and will use the change He allowed to give you the abundance He has planned for you. The grief and loss process is a worthy and noble endeavor. Please ponder this idea; many times God has to remove things in order to make or create space to bring the new or better thing. In the words of Selwyn Hughes, "God always gives the best to those who leave the choice to him." [10]

The Serenity Prayer

God, give me grace to accept with serenity
the things that cannot be changed,
Courage to change the things
which should be changed,
and the Wisdom to distinguish
the one from the other.
Living one day at a time,
Enjoying one moment at a time,
Accepting hardship as a pathway to peace,
Taking, as Jesus did,
This sinful world as it is,
Not as I would have it,
Trusting that You will make all things right,
If I surrender to Your will,
So that I may be reasonably happy in this life,
And supremely happy with You forever in the next.
Amen. [11]

Reflection Questions:

1. Which of the maladaptive coping skills do you find yourself using most frequently?

2. In your childhood family, which of these negative coping skills were used most often by your parents and siblings? What do you see your family continue to practice today?

3. What are your favorite, or most *familiar*, maladaptive coping skills?

4. How are they working for you? How are they getting in your way?

5. Are you willing to go through the dying process and "let go" of negative coping skills?

6. On a scale from 1 to 10, what is your level of resistance to "let go" of those negative coping skills?

7. What is your greatest fear when contemplating or deciding to die to those "negative coping skills"?

8. How much condemnation are you experiencing as a result of practicing maladaptive coping skills?

9. Are any of the negative coping skills you are dealing with a result of the "two types of death"? Or are the maladaptive coping skills learned from childhood

further exacerbated or concretized by the dying process? For example: You've never had a problem with alcohol, but you now find yourself having two or three glasses a night at home alone since your last child went away to college, or you are now single for the first time. Maybe you grew up in a family that practiced intellectualizing and denial, but you never really noticed it until you had to face several health issues that became life-threatening because of those maladaptive coping skills.

10. List the stages of grief and loss, then journal and talk with someone about each stage. It is helpful, while resolving the loss, to take advantage of rituals and the support of others.

    Shock: This is usually a relatively short stage. Shock is in the first couple of hours and moves straight into denial.

    Denial: It may sound or look like the following: I keep thinking my boyfriend/girlfriend just needs time, so I continue to look at my phone or email to see if they are communicating with me; I'm thinking my husband/wife is just going through an angry phase, and they're really not divorcing me; I know the doctor's report is a false, the test was wrong.

    Bargaining: I keep going over what happened, I know I could have done it differently, and I'm just beating myself up because it could have been different. I'll keep asking God what I can do to stop this from happening. *If I could just to back to yesterday.*

Anger: What does anger feel like to me, how is it manifesting in my life, and are there any defense mechanisms I am using to manage anger? For example, I am so angry about this loss that I am withdrawing and not wanting to be social, or my anger is becoming passive-aggressive. Maybe my anger is more overt, and I find myself slamming doors or throwing things. It could be that I'm swearing a lot and snapping at people. What am I the most angry about? "I am so angry I have to forgive! This was not supposed to happen to me, this is so unfair. God, where are you?" It is very helpful to write angry letters to whomever you feel any anger toward, no matter how small. These letters are to vent, not to send.

Sadness/mourning: I have stopped eating; I don't want to get out of bed; showering seems insurmountable. I am crying at the drop of a hat; everything hurts.

Acceptance/Forgiveness: I can finally go to where we had our first date. This stage comes and goes, each time coming to a deeper level of acceptance, peace, and forgiveness. It is helpful here to journal about forgiveness of yourself, others, or God—whomever you feel could have changed or stopped the outcome you are having to heal from.

Chapter 6

GOD IS DOING A NEW THING

"Jesus, overcome me, as You have overcome the world."
– Cinthia Hiett

I'm hopeful that by now, I've shown you that God wants to, can, and will complete a good work in you if you allow Him to. Actually, He will do it anyway. The difference is that when I use my free will to overcome my self-will, the process is much more collaborative, meaningful, and inspiring. He wants to take you through a dying process so you can be the best version of yourself—the one He created you to be.

Perhaps you're thinking, and you wouldn't be the first, "This stinks. Why should I have to go through a difficult, painful dying process? Why couldn't God create me a little closer to what He had in mind in the first place?"

Well, friend, He did, in the beginning.
Let's consider God's first human creation:

Adam.

Adam's Choice

What do we know about Adam? This first man had everything he needed, including daily fellowship with his Creator and, eventually, with an ideal companion and helper named Eve. He ruled over the animals; he walked in a beautiful garden. The world was fresh and new, and disease, pestilence, sorrow, sadness, decay, strife, death—the things we now face on a daily basis—had not yet come into play. Even if Adam wasn't destined to be perfect, the world around him was.

We don't know how long Adam lived without sin and whether the time was measured in days or years. Either way, can you imagine living without sin? No guilt, shame, condemnation, or compulsive feelings—not to mention the things listed above that sin unleashed on the world. What a life that would be! If I could live a single day without sin, or the effects of it, it would be the best day in history since Adam's downfall.

We know that Adam sinned. What kind of sin was it? A classic: the sin of using free will to choose self-will over God's will. We do this all the time and think nothing of it; but God did not, and does not, think it's nothing. He does forgive us and love us anyway, but our sin is *not nothing*. No, sin brought entirely new things into this world, none of them good, and it also brought entirely new feelings.

Adam's first feelings after his sin were fear and shame. Have you ever thought about the fact that we were not originally designed for negative feelings produced from sin? Sin brought them. Did sin also bring new feelings to God? Well, maybe.

If you're a parent, consider the first time the child you lovingly reared scrunched up her precious little face and shouted "NO!" to your request that she please pick up her toys. Who is this person, and what has she done with your little cherub?!? It's a surprising moment when your child first disobeys.

Of course, there are also the previously-undiscovered positive feelings, too: for instance, at the first sweet, juicy little baby kiss on your cheek. When sin entered the world through Adam, it certainly did a new thing, but not necessarily a good one.

The shame and fear Adam felt came from experiencing knowledge too soon. In fact, the whole creation was shamed; we were never intended to feel fear, doubt, uncertainty, anxiety, insecurity, and all the rest. Creation was launched into a perpetuating cycle of fear, shame, guilt, and sin, creating separation from self, God, and others. What's more, out of shame and guilt come a sense of powerlessness, which gives rise to anger and pride: two emotions that can feel empowering. We seek to manage all of these feelings; but, more often than not, it is through unhealthy, hedonistic, and self-medicating behaviors.

So we see that when Adam and Eve were exposed to knowledge beyond their limits, they experienced evil. Prior to this, we could say they were in heaven, feeling only bliss, joy, contentment, meaning, purpose, confidence, security, and, most of all, *love*. With the advent of knowledge and exposure to evil, humankind "fell into hell." As a result God had to place us in time in order to "stop the drop" into hell. While He began His work of rescue, He flexed his "strong arm" to stop deployment into eternal separation from himself as well as eternal separation from our best self within ourselves.

> *Was there no champion to come forward? None found he, and his heart misgave him. And so his own arm must bring the deliverance he intended, his own faithfulness held him to it.* (Isaiah 59:16 KNOX)

He is allowing a "redo," or a "mulligan," to say so glibly! This is the second choice if we will take it: a do-over. Some welcome this opportunity with open arms; others stick to Adam's choice, their own self-will, and bring death upon themselves and their world.

God is giving every human that has ever been created the opportunity to undo "Adams choice" if they so desire. Not only do we have a choice, but God will also help us make the decision and stay the course—even though every day we all relapse back into choosing sin and death. Every time we do manage to die to self-will and choose God's will, however, God heals us from sin's infection. And when we ask God to dwell in us, He accepts and rejoices in the request. He is willing to live with whatever feelings we may be experiencing—even the negative ones—and become our heaven in the midst of what would be hell. This can be your choice, too, if in the little decisions you face, minute by minute, you choose *life*.

> This day I call the heavens and the earth as witnesses against you that I have set before you life and death, blessings and curses. Now choose life, so that you and your children may live. (Deuteronomy 30:19 NIV)

Despite these wise words, and many others, plenty of us choose death and sin many times a day. Sometimes, for a lifetime. When we choose sin, and therefore death, we must repent, and we will receive forgiveness from a gracious and merciful God. But we also have to receive forgiveness from someone else: ourselves. We must resist the temptation to walk out the second part of Adam's choice, in which we experience shame, guilt, and condemnation, and the only way to do this is to accept God's forgiveness and also offer ourselves the same forgiveness that we know God offers us (i.e., practicing the love chapter toward ourselves). So often, many of us lean strongly toward condemning ourselves, which leads us away from the center of ourselves where God resides. As a result, we're again trapped in death, now experiencing "hell." God invites us back into His presence, healing us with love, patience, kindness, and mercy. All of these make us stronger and better able to choose life next time. He does this for us continually; our entire life story here on earth is supported and protected until we are "home" and free from Adam's choice.

Jesus had this down pat. In everything, He abdicated to God's will. He knew that to continually die to self-will and choose God's will was the way to an abundant life. He also knew that to choose self-will would separate him from God, which would ultimately lead to death—hence the death of Jesus through the process of "giving up his spirit."

Not My will, but Yours, be done. (Luke 22:42 NKJV)

> I tell you the truth, the Son can do nothing by himself; he can do only what he sees His Father doing, because whatever the Father does the Son also does. (John 5:19 NIV)

What is God's will? It's this:

> My prayer is not for them alone. I pray also for those who will believe in me through their message, that all of them may be one, Father, just as you are in me and I am in you. May they also be in us so that the world may believe that you have sent me. I have given them the glory that you gave me, that they may be one as we are one—I in them and you in me—so that they may be brought to complete unity. Then the world will know that you sent me and have loved them even as you have loved me. (John 17:20–23 NIV)

God is willing and wanting to be such a big part of our lives; He actually wants to be inseparable from us. Believe it or not, He even wants to inhabit the ugly places where sin or regret or guilt pervades our very souls. He still sees our original design and the way He created us to be. And in fact, He wants to complete the "good work He has begun in us" (Philippians 1:6), a work that is fully integrated, fully alive, fully human, and fully divine. And this is what is revealed in "The Lord's Prayer." Jesus says, *"Your Kingdom come, your will be done, on earth, as it is in heaven"* Matthew 6:10 (NIV). My life, my body is an entity God must invade and, indeed, possess. Just as He is bringing his kingdom to the world as a whole, He is also working on our own little world. Jesus says, *"In this world you will have trouble. But take heart! I have overcome the world"* (John 16:33 NIV). So I ask God daily, "Please, Lord, in your mercy, overcome me, as you have overcome the world."

This type of intimate relationship is the only way to pull us back to our original design; how can we be who we're meant to be without the help of our Creator? Peter allowed this process through great humility; after he denied Christ three times, he was reconciled through repentance and went on to fulfill the great destiny God had designed for him. How often do we miss our great and ultimate design due to a lack of humility?

Our choices are our own—each one is unique to each one of us, whether we choose life or death. When we choose life, we "undo" the remnant of Adam's choice that plagues our mortal bodies. To do this, we must use our free will to surrender our self-will to God's will. The only "formula" we have for dying to self is our own individual way to choose life.

Our unique, one-time-occurring life is full of billions or trillions of tiny choices, medium choices, and huge opportunities through all the moments and seasons of a lifetime. And in each of these choices, we are able to undo Adam's choice by following God's will instead of our own.

This becomes *your choice* when you can ask and allow God to undo Adam's legacy in you by choosing God's will, choosing His way.

> Today I have given you the choice between **life** and death, between blessings and curses. Now I call on heaven and earth to witness the choice you make. Oh, that you would **choose life**, so that you and your descendants might live! (Deuteronomy 30:19 NLT, emphasis added)

But you can't do it on your own. This is why Jesus lives in us. He always chooses life; He helps us die to ourselves, as He did, so that we might live as He does (see Romans 6:1–7, Galatians 2:20).

> "You were taught, with regard to your former way of life, to put off your old self, which is being corrupted by its deceitful desires; to be made new in the attitude of your minds; and to put on the new self, created to be like God in true righteousness and holiness." (Ephesians 4:22–24 NIV)

His power is working within us to will and do his good work (See Ephesians 1:9, Philippians 1:6).

> "Think about this. Wrap your minds around it. This is serious business, rebels. Take it to heart. Remember your history, your long and rich history. I am GOD, the only God you've had or ever will have—incomparable, irreplaceable— From the very beginning telling you what the ending will be, All along letting you in on what is going to happen, Assuring you, 'I'm in this for the long haul, I'll do exactly what I set out to do,' Calling that eagle, Cyrus, out of the east,
> from a far country the man I chose to help me. I've said it, and I'll most certainly do it. I've planned it, so it's as good as done." (Isaiah 46:10-11 MSG)

Does all this seem overwhelming? The truth is we are infected with sin. Fortunately, God understands that sick people, captive people, don't always choose well. They often make choices based simply on a desire to survive the moment, rather than a choice that would cause them to thrive. POW's, or anyone who has been held captive for any length of time, often don't know how to live free even when they have been freed. Many times they unconsciously choose strategies that are based in survival which usually bring more bondage.

This is why the psalmist says, *"I've been out of step with you for a long time, in the wrong since before I was born. What you're after is truth from the inside out. Enter me, then; conceive a new, true life"* Psalm 51:5-6 (MSG).

This is not to expose or shame us in a condemnatory manner, but to offer choice in the captive and sick parts of ourselves. In the areas that we are unaware of, or have separated ourselves from, He wants to help us manage our negative feelings rather than being held hostage or imprisoned by them, and then choose sin as a way to medicate those feelings. God so beautifully encourages us by saying, *"He will respond to the prayer of the destitute, he will not despise their plea"* in Psalm 102:17(NIV).

Now, it's time to focus on a life of freedom—of the good work God can do, and is doing, in you.

What is this New Thing?

As I mentioned earlier in this book, there's no step-by-step dying process. It's unique to each person, and it leads to a uniquely abundant life. But there are some practices and thought patterns that are likely to help you discover what it is that's killing you, allow God to put an end to it, and embark on your abundant life. Take a look:

1. Recognize that the solution is life on God's terms.
Your dying process will not be successful unless you realize that it's on God's terms. Not yours. It will feel strange and different, and, most likely, extremely uncomfortable at times. It is not the route you would take if left to your own devices. The goal—the abundant life you've been craving—might look vastly different than anything you'd plan for yourself (just look at the difference between Peter's abundant life and Job's). This is not your will—it's God's, and you must surrender to God's terms. He's given everything to free you from the effects of living in condemnation. Take some time to meditate and integrate the following truth expressed through God's Word:

With the arrival of Jesus, the Messiah, that fateful dilemma is resolved. Those who enter into Christ's being-here-for-us no longer have to live under a continuous, low-lying black cloud. A new power is in operation. The Spirit of life in Christ, like a strong wind, has magnificently cleared the air, freeing you from a fated lifetime of brutal tyranny at the hands of sin and death. God went for the jugular when he sent his own Son. He didn't deal with the problem as something remote and unimportant. In his Son, Jesus, he personally took on the human condition, entered the disordered mess of struggling humanity in order to set it right once and for all.

The law code, weakened as it always was by fractured human nature, could never have done that. The law always ended up being used as a Band-Aid on sin instead of a deep healing of it. And now what the law code asked for but we couldn't deliver is accomplished as we, instead of redoubling our own efforts, simply embrace what the Spirit is doing in us. (Romans 8:1–4 MSG)

You might inwardly writhe in agony, or trepidation, at the idea of surrendering your will to God's, but the benefits are overwhelming. Nothing is impossible for God; no situation you find yourself in, nor any reality you have created for yourself, is unsolvable. No bad decision is too hard for God to redeem or to correct. God's "arm is not too short," as we see in the following discourse between Moses and God, as well as Jeremiah and the Lord.

> The LORD answered Moses, "Is the LORD's arm too short? Now you will see whether or not what I say will come true for you." (Numbers 11:23 NIV)

Listen to the verbal discourse as Jeremiah responds to the Lord. He starts by saying what he "knows" is true:

> "Ah, Sovereign LORD, you have made the heavens and the earth by your great power and outstretched arm. Nothing is too hard for you." (Jeremiah 32:17 NIV)

The Lord responds back to Jeremiah in verses 26–27 by saying:

> Then the word of the LORD came to Jeremiah:

"I am the LORD, the God of all mankind. Is anything too hard for me?" (Jeremiah 32:26-27 NIV)

God is the solution for your life—but the solution must be on His terms. Are you ready to use your free will to surrender your self-will to His will?

2. **Let Christ lead; beware of Satan.**
"I have been crucified with Christ [in Him I have shared His crucifixion]; it is no longer I who live, but Christ (the Messiah) lives in me; and the life I now live in the body I live by faith in (by adherence to and reliance on and complete trust in) the Son of God, Who loved me and gave Himself up for me." (Galatians 2:20 AMP)

In your dying process, it's vital that you keep Christ as your example. It is easier said than done—after all, the lures of Satan and his devilish plans are tempting, to say the least. Satan knows that Jesus conquered death and in that there is subsequent life. He is all too aware that there is life in the dying process (remember the C.S. Lewis quote, "the cure for death is dying"?). This is why he discourages the process so vehemently. He would have us shrink from this noble endeavor and continue as the "living dead," becoming more hedonistic in the management of our pain. And he's an expert at convincing people to stray from the path, God's way, by backtracking or stalling out along the way. No, Jesus himself must be our leader, our example, our rescuer, and our guide. Take a look at 1 Peter 2:24 (MSG): *"This is the kind of life you've been invited into, the kind of life Christ lived. He suffered everything that came his way so you would know that it could be done, and also know how to do it, step-by-step."* Jesus never did one thing wrong, not once said anything amiss.

They called Him every name in the book, and He said nothing back. He suffered in silence, content to let God set things right. He used His servant body to carry our sins to the cross, so we could be rid of sin, free to live the right way. His wounds became our healing. We were lost sheep with no idea who we were or where we were going. Now we're named and kept for good by the Shepherd of our souls.

The enemy is happy to partner with us in any way that would take the focus off of Jesus and pull us apart from our Savior. He'll work to convince us to die to the wrong things or keep the wrong things alive, so that we become ineffective for this world and for ourselves. This only leads to a living death—not a crucified life—and renders Christ's death for us useless, which is the last thing we want.

On the other hand, the best weapon we have against the enemy of our souls is to *"die to the right things."* Our willingness to die, as stated in Galatians 2:20, is kryptonite to Satan, because he knows that when we die to our own will, we are then able to truly love and be loved. And we know that love covers a multitude of sin (1 Peter 4:8), and love never fails (1 Corinthians 13:8).

The other pitfall we have to watch out for is that of relying too heavily on the world around us to lead in our dying process. While it's certainly helpful to seek wisdom from trusted people, to rely exclusively on the church, a friend, a tradition, etc., could very likely lead us down the wrong path. For instance, it's easy to fall into a legalistic approach—trying to "act right" on the outside, only to discover that our sick and wounded insides soon find us out and call our bluff. God realizes, however, that we are inside out, upside down, and backward. The dying process puts us right side up, facing forward, and right side in. We are now standing upright, moving in the right direction, with our insides manifesting the right behaviors outside. I say so often to myself and to my clients, "If you don't do the internal work, the external won't work!" So it begins by changing our inside, not changing our appearance and hoping the rest will follow. Remember that God knew we would be unable to conquer our own death and sin, so He sent Jesus. He's not expecting us to save ourselves.

> "Let us hold unswervingly to the hope we profess, for he who promised is faithful." (Hebrews 10:23 NIV)

3. Ask the Holy Spirit to reveal what is killing us, and what needs to change.

Adam's choice brought sin into the world; we now have a fallen nature. We addressed earlier the concept of the second type of death: "dying to the things that are killing me." I've found in my practice that there are a number of common things; these are things that are common to humans regardless of social strata, skin color, intelligence, gender, etc. These are the sins common to all man—not unique sins, just unique in the way they may be stealing, destroying, and killing us. It's vital to understand, however, that seeking your personal, necessary area of change is more than reading down a list and checking a couple of boxes. After all, we don't always know what the future holds, and where our deepest insecurities lie. We are often blind to the truths (both positive and negative) that our friends and families may see but that seem to elude our awareness. We must, therefore, be willing to humbly ask the Holy Spirit to reveal to us how we are participating in death, maybe even pursuing things that are actively killing the authentic person God has created and subsequently died for. We are asking the Holy Spirit, and whomever we consider to be "safe" individuals, to support us in addressing what is true about ourselves. What is upside down, inside out, and backwards in our lives? What needs to die in me, or better yet, what is killing me, which is causing me to be living dead? All the time we should be recognizing and trusting that we are not living under that dark cloud of condemnation; but rather, we have the God of all love sitting right next to us. Not only is He without disgust or shock at our situation, but He also has a uniquely marvelous way out of this valley of death that we have found ourselves within.

    Prayerfully consider these things that are common to all humans, which steal our uniqueness and relegate us to "commoners." Ask the Holy Spirit to reveal what needs to change in your life, and then be open to His answer. I want you to consider two categories of sin as a way to help identify and clarify what the Holy Spirit *currently* wants to address. Thankfully the Lord does not show us everything all at once; we would be too discouraged. Instead He "doses" out the truth regarding our sin only in a quantity that will set us free. Too much truth would be overwhelming and put us into bondage. The enemy of our souls loves to use the "truth" to bind us up and load us up with the heavy burden of our sin. Jesus says to us that His "burden is light and his yoke is easy" (Matthew 11:30. God tells us the truth to set us free; Satan uses the facts to condemn us," and we are NEVER to listen to the enemy in regards our life. Even if Satan is speaking the truth regarding our sin, he is using the truth to lie to us about who we are and how valuable we are. The work that Jesus would have us do regarding ourselves is never intended to overload us, but to properly strengthen and free us. Condemnation is a heavy burden to bear, and it never emanates from our Savior. We have addressed many unique and varying phenomena to which we are to die; we now are left to address our basic human condition, this being the fallen nature.

What is "common" to all humans? It is a fact that we have an enduring propensity to deeply desire, long for, and enjoy those things that are not only contrary to God's original design but also become an infective toxin, a cancer to our very souls. Oftentimes in first world countries these common conditions are culturally rationalized, accepted, and now even revered. Let's take a moment and consider the long-time and enduring, historically-viable categorizations of these issues common to all mankind regardless of race, religion, gender, strata, or culture: the "seven deadly sins." We cannot have a book on *dying to self* and overlook the most common issues killing us. The devotion and ongoing commitment to resist and battle these common issues is crucial when seeking the abundant life. The abundance God desires for us is always stolen, destroyed, and killed when these sins are in abundance. The enemy of our soul always has these temptations in his arsenal as a way to kill, steal, and destroy not only the abundant life God has planned for you, but the one He died for you to have.

Back to Basics

This can get a little thorny and quite unpleasant. You are now probably saying, "As if I don't already have enough to contend with!" I can relate and concur; when I am addressing these issues, I just want to say, "Ow, ow, ow!" However, we must continue to trust the love and commitment God has displayed toward His creation. He wants to rid us of anything that gets in the way of experiencing an abundant life. But it really doesn't feel good and requires that we avail ourselves of the love and courage God gives us as we look at these together.

The seven deadly sins aren't necessarily a list in

the Bible, although there are several references throughout the Scriptures that have been instrumental in the development of the "big seven." They date back to the early church and have been part of church tradition. Proverbs 6:16-19 and Galatians 5:19-21 are often cited as lists, the seven deadly sins being a derivation of these; at other points in the Bible all seven of these sins are described. I do not see these sins as bigger or worse than transgressing the other laws of the Bible—these being the Ten Commandments and the greater laws given to us by Christ in the New Testament. These sins are the cancer to our souls, affecting our ability to obey any of the "lifestyle" laws proscribed in Scripture. If regularly practiced, they become perfected, killing the original design and taking up more and more space in our hearts and minds, and eventually killing the body. These sins are considered "deadly," and for good reason. If the enemy can't negatively affect us from the outside, he will attempt to destroy us from within. Please be comforted, understanding that you are in good company; we all commit these sins in some form every day. This is what makes the crucifixion and resurrection so very needed and beautiful. What are the "seven deadly sins"? This is a very cryptic topic, and I would encourage you to study them in more depth as you continue in this process of "living."

PRIDE: This sin is considered the sin from which all other sins arise; it is also known as vanity. This is an overdependence on oneself, the tendency toward competition, and comparing and contrasting oneself with others. This sin interferes with the recognition of God's grace and the ability to receive and accept it as love and grace. "Legalism" and a "works mentality" emanate and thrive from the individual struggling with pride. The cure or remedy is *humility*.

ENVY: This is a compelling desire, sometimes to the point of obsession, of others' traits, status, belongings, lifestyle, appearance, talents, achievements, situations, etc. so as to change our mood and our ability to extend grace and happiness when others achieve or receive good things. The cure or remedy is *kindness*.

GLUTTONY: A compulsion, or inordinate desire, for more than one needs or requires, i.e., "If a little is good, more is better." This struggle is one of "stopping." It's filling the void in our soul with vices or things. It is the struggle with insatiability. The cure or remedy for this sin is the practice of *abstinence*.

LUST: This is a disproportionate or uncurbed craving

for the pleasures of the body, usually associated with sexual sin. This is often a relationship disorder; it manifests in the inability to get one's needs met in a healthy manner. The cure or remedy for this is *chastity*.

ANGER: We are not talking about appropriate anger, but the anger that is oftentimes emanating from wrath. Anger and wrath may come from immaturity, pride, selfishness, and self-pity. This type of sin indulges first in anger and spurns love. The cure or remedy is *patience*.

GREED: This sin is also called covetousness or avarice. It is a desire for material wealth and gain and ignores the spiritual realm. Greed is a great temptation, and Satan is the master of rationalizing the lines a person may cross in order to acquire and achieve the wealth that never satisfies. The remedy or cure is *liberality*.

SLOTH: This sin is characterized by a resistance, or all-out avoidance, of physical or spiritual work. There is a tendency to let others do what needs to be done, an unwillingness to participate in living, and a resistance to exert oneself. The cure or remedy for sloth is *diligence*.

A very effective way to understand and organize these sins scripturally is seen in the passage out of 1 John 2:16: *For all that is in the world, the **lust of the flesh** and the **lust of the eyes** and the **pride of life**, is not of the Father but is of the world* (NKJV, emphasis added). John talks about the seven deadly sins through three basic categories or types: the lust of the flesh (gluttony, lust, sloth), the lust of the eyes (greed), and the pride of life (pride, envy, anger). Overcoming these things should, and will, be our life's work.

Furthermore, these sins might be categorized by two different natures, coupled by two differing ways in which they are committed. The first two categories of sin will be either covert or overt in nature. The word overt means that nothing is hidden; it is apparent, obvious, public, undisguised, or visible. Covert, on the other hand, is used to describe something clandestine, cloaked, disguised, secret, or hidden. The two ways in which sin is committed is through the act of sin through "commission" or "omission." More simply put, this means I sin by doing something, or I sin because I didn't do something. What might be some examples?

Drinking alcohol and driving is an *overt* sin of *commission*. "It's obvious that I am doing something wrong." Having a "closet" drinking problem is an *overt* sin done in a *covert* way through an act of commission

(Always remember there is no condemnation. The sin is not that the person is struggling with an addiction; the sin is the behaviors that manifest from the addiction and/or not taking responsibility for the addiction). Not paying my tithe can be an example of a sin of *omission*, which is done in a *covert* manner. I sin because I didn't do something, *and* it was not obvious to others. What happens when I have a covert sin in my life (a sin that is hidden even to me), but is done in an overt manner (obvious to others)? What would that look like? This might look like pride, gossip, lack of boundaries, lack of self-control, etc., and then it may be a sin of commission or omission. Take some time and ask the Lord to reveal to you the areas of omission, commission, covert and overt sins that are killing you in any combination thereof.

Most of us don't need to be told when we are sinning; the reason that we are taking time to identify common sins is simply because this area of our lives is continuously exploited by the enemy and our own denial and justification. We get so very tired of "looking" at our sin and failing. As a result we tend to minimize and "work around" the sin. We end up being "dead" to our sin in the wrong way. Instead of dying to the sin, we are just dead in it. But we are not to lose hope; God knew what we would be facing and always has a way.

> "I have the right to do anything," you say—but not everything is beneficial. "I have the right to do anything"—but not everything is constructive.
>
> (1 Corinthians 10:23 NIV)

God is not interested in just abiding by the law; He wants us to live fully and completely. So when I look at the "thing that is killing me that needs to die," I must recognize that, although it may be permissible, it might not be constructive or beneficial to me. Whether it's lawful, or moral, or not, and whether or not others are able to do it, beneficially, *is it beneficial for me?*

To find your answer, you'll need to look a little deeper and press in further with the Lord to discover your unique make-up. Ask your Creator to tell you what is stopping you from being you and being all He has for you. This is different from inquiring what is allowed or condoned by religion or culture, or even by your family and close friends—in fact, it's often a cop-out and stumbling block to allow these paradigms to dictate your choices and habits. Please, don't get me wrong: the Ten Commandments are a great place to start, just as my cultural norms may be a helpful, or necessary, starting point. It's clear, however, that even if something is constructive for me, I have the responsibility to take into account how my lifestyle affects the people with whom I live and interact. I must have the mind of Christ, the guidance of the Holy Spirit, and a working knowledge of my Creator. If not, I will fall into the trap of legalism, or be codependent, or some awful combination of both!

It may seem daunting to uncover what's *really* holding you back, but the Holy Spirit will help you—just ask.

4. **Don't be the "Lone Ranger."**
Behold, all you [enemies of your own selves] who attempt to kindle your own fires [and work out your own plans of salvation], who surround and gird yourselves with momentary sparks, darts, and firebrands that you set aflame!—walk by the light of your self-made fire and of the sparks that you have kindled [for yourself, if you will]! But this shall you have from My hand: you shall lie down in grief and in torment. (Isaiah 50:11 AMP)

Mrs. Charles E. Cowman's March 30th devotional in *Streams in the Desert*, refers to this passage and says, "What a solemn warning to those who walk in darkness and yet who try to help themselves out into the light. They are represented as kindling fire, and compassing themselves with sparks. What does this mean? Why, it means that when we are in darkness the temptation is to find a way without trusting in the Lord and relying upon Him. Instead of letting Him help us out, we try to help ourselves out. We seek the light of nature and get the advice of friends. We try the conclusions of our reason and might almost be tempted to accept a way of deliverance, which would not be God at all.

Beloved, do not try to get out of a dark place, except in God's time and in God's way. The time of trouble is meant to teach you lessons that you sorely need. Premature deliverance may frustrate God's work of grace in your life. Just commit the whole situation to Him. Be willing to abide in darkness (death) so long as you have His presence. Remember that it is better to walk in the dark with God than to walk alone in the light." [12]

We all do it. We all try to scramble out of tough situations on our own terms, and of our own will. We find our own way rather than trusting God, even turning to friends, the Internet, and our own reasoning rather than prayer. And we might even find a solution that's workable except for one thing: it's not God's will.

It's far better to wait patiently for God's work to be revealed. Don't crack open the chrysalis before the butterfly has a chance to form; and resist the urge to set a time limit. The more you take the reins, the further out of control your life will race. Remember that unless you're directed by God's hand, helping yourself is no help at all.

But that's not to say that we need to walk the road entirely alone, and that we can never ask for help. Cease meddling with God's plans and will. You touch anything of His, and you mar the work. You move the hands of a clock to suit you, but you do not change the time; so you may hurry the unfolding of God's will, you harm and do not help the work. You can open a rosebud, but you spoil the flower. Leave all to Him. Hands down. Thy will, not mine. (Stephen Merritt).

In the last point, I wrote about how important it is to not simply follow the norms and standards of your culture, family, friends, or church when it comes to seeking out what needs to die, or how to follow God's dying process for you. There is, however, great value in considering the wisdom that can be gleaned from these fields. I've noticed that the people I see feel they can't be honest about their needs. They tell me because they can't bring up the subject to their friends, their spouse, or their family. They don't want to tell their pastor because of what the church will think, and so they tell me. It's confidential, just like what God affords us. Sometimes our pride won't let us be open and honest to the people we know, sometimes we are not safe people for one another, and sometimes both. But when *I* am the only person people feel comfortable talking to about the "big" stuff, one thing quickly becomes clear: we are dying from loneliness, and our community is failing.

Do we always have to do this "life" thing alone? Perhaps not. In fact, we shouldn't; we always have God as our confidante, sounding board, and friend. Many of us would also have willing—if not imperfect—ears if we could let go of our own fear and pride enough to accept people in their process. We must trust that God sees what we see, hears what we hear, and cares about what we care about! Your relationship with yourself directly affects how you relate to others. When I am practicing the love chapter within myself, I am much better able to extend this love to others. If I can't find "safe" people in my community to share with, I need to start being a "safe" person to the people in my life. Change must start with me—that is the Jesus way. If you can, listen to the people around you, whatever is said, and the things that are unsaid, too. Test every bit of it against what the Holy Spirit is whispering to you as well. Ask for the truth to be revealed about yourself first, then others, realizing, hopefully, that that's exactly what you might get.

5. Celebrate the harvest!

This is the way God put it: "They found grace out in the

desert, these people who survived the killing. Israel, out looking for a place to rest, met God out looking for them!" God told them:

"I've never quit loving you and never will. Expect love, love, and more love! And so now I'll start over with you and build you up again, dear virgin (make us new again) Israel. You'll resume your singing, grabbing tambourines and joining the dance. You'll go back to your old work of planting vineyards on the Samaritan hillsides, and sit back and enjoy the fruit—oh, how you'll enjoy those harvests!" (Jeremiah 31:2–6 MSG)

And now, God, do it again—bring rains to our drought-stricken lives. So those who planted their crops in despair will shout hurrahs at the harvest, so those who went off with heavy hearts will come home laughing, with armloads of blessing. (Psalm 126:4–6 MSG)

And so God gave Israel the entire land that he had solemnly vowed to give to their ancestors. They took possession of it and made themselves at home in it. And God gave them rest on all sides, as he had also solemnly vowed to their ancestors. Not a single one of their enemies was able to stand up to them—God handed over all their enemies to them. Not one word failed from all the good words God spoke to the house of Israel.

Everything came out right. (Joshua 21:43–45 MSG, emphasis added)

As you see God's changes at work in you, and as you witness the death of whatever it is that has you in its grasp, take note of how far you've come. Ask the Holy Spirit regularly for encouragement and to show you the changes in your life, your patterns, and your behaviors. What new thing is God revealing to you that He has done in your life? Prepare to be amazed!

At the same time, be aware that others before you have turned back—and lost everything. Resist this unique kind of temptation and go only confidently forward. The old has gone, the new is here! Enjoy it!

But Lot's wife looked back, and she became a pillar of salt. (Genesis 19:26 NIV)

> When the Day arrives and you're out working in the yard, don't run into the house to get anything. And if you're out in the field, don't go back and get your coat. Remember what happened to Lot's wife! If you grasp and cling to life on your terms, you'll lose it, but if you let that life go, you'll get life on God's terms. (Luke 17:31–33 MSG)

God has promised abundant harvests to His people, and He will deliver to those who accept Him. And what can be more joyful than a harvest after a year's worth of hard work, perseverance, and painful labor? When you see your harvest, whatever form it may take, celebrate! God will be celebrating with you.

6. Empathize with fellow travelers.
"I don't want you to become part of something that reduces you to less than yourself. And you can't have it both ways, banqueting with the Master one day and slumming with demons the next. Besides, the Master won't put up with it. He wants us—all or nothing. Do you think you can get off with anything less? Looking at it one way, you could say, "Anything goes. Because of God's immense generosity and grace, we don't have to dissect and scrutinize every action to see if it will pass muster." But the point is not to just get by. We want to live well, but our foremost efforts should be to help others live well. (1 Corinthians 10:21–24 MSG)

One of the things I've found that I love most about my career is "entering into the fellowship of suffering." It is a miraculous aspect of the human condition, in that, listening, empathizing, and commiserating are some of the most remarkably healing and connective aspects of humanity. I'd encourage everyone to enter into these when the situation arises. This means that even when your "battle" is won, the work isn't over. God's plan isn't so limited. He desires and intends for us to look outward, to use what we've learned and the love and grace He's given us to help others on similar journeys.

Every time God brings us safely through a trial, we learn more about our lives. And we're also given a greater capacity to understand the trials of others and to empathize, as well as sympathize, with them. You'll find that anyone who has suffered much, but has been brought to safety with God's hand, knows what suffering really means and is gentler on the rest of humankind. The more we've suffered, the less judgmental we should be, and the more helpful become to others.

He comforted us so that we may comfort others. We need to let our lives be inspiring to each other. I tell my patients frequently: God is not healing you so you can go and "have a happy life." He is healing you so that you can inspire, encourage, and strengthen others. This is so that the work of our Lord is complete, His good work—the ultimate healing and unification of the body of Christ. That we would lose not one!

What is your part in this destiny, the destiny of being a believer, a follower of Christ? Don't take the death of Christ for granted. Why did He die for you? Specifically for you? Beyond His great love for you, what was the point of saving you? There is a reason you have come to know Him, there is a reason you were created, and there is a unique point to your life. You must pursue it, you must find it, and you must require God reveal it so that you may live it out!

> All things are lawful, but not all things are profitable. All things are lawful, but not all things edify. Let no one seek his own good, but that of his neighbor.
> (1 Corinthians 10:23–24 NASB)

> All praise goes to God, Father of our Lord Jesus, the Anointed One. He is the Father of compassion, the God of all comfort. He consoles us as we endure the pain and hardship of life so that we may draw from His comfort and share it with others in their own struggles. For even as His suffering continues to flood over us, through the Anointed we experience the wealth of His comfort just the same. (2 Corinthians 1:3–5 VOICE)

"For I know the plans I have for you," says the Eternal, "plans for peace, not evil, to give you a future and hope—*never forget that*. At that time, you will call out for Me, *and I will hear*. You will pray, and I will listen. You will look for Me intently, and you will find Me." (Jeremiah 29:11–13 VOICE)

This is our commission: to "be our on best version," to know what is *constructive* for us, to use our trials to comfort others, to trust God's plans for us, and to allow our dying process to ultimately help others connect more deeply with God and become their own best version. If we look to our ultimate role model, Jesus Christ, we see that this parallels His ministry perfectly.

Are you willing to be an extension of Christ, someone who is helping to un-do Adam's choice? Every time you choose God's will and God's way by using your free will to die to self-will, you help undo the fallen-ness of man, of all God's creation.

As we end this chapter, please be encouraged and know you are loved through the following exhortation I wrote.

An Exhortation

Your God is never anxious,
Your God is never worried,
Your God is never surprised,
Your God is never shocked,
Your God never looks upon you with disdain,
Nor is He ever disgusted or despising of you . . .

Rather, Your God loves, all the time,
Your God shows mercy, all the time,
Your God shows everlasting patience, all the time,
Your God shows understanding, all the time,
Your God is gracious, all the time,
On this you can depend, for this is true, all the time
For your God is Truth, and truth cannot lie.

Cinthia Hiett, 10/14/12

Notes

1. Young, Sarah. 2004. "May 5th entry." *Jesus Calling: Devotions for Every Day of the Year,* 132. Nashville, TN: Thomas Nelson Publishers.
2. This is a saying that I have created. It is used on my website, Facebook page, business cards, etc. It is the idea behind all I do and teach.
3. Paraphrased from *Man's Search for Meaning* by Victor E. Frankl. 1959. Boston, MA: Beacon Press.
4. Homer-Dixon, Homera. 1996. "February 19th entry." *Streams in the Desert,* edited by L.B. Cowman. Grand Rapids, MI: Zondervan.
5. Lewis, C.S. 1958. *The Pilgrim's Regress,* 172. Grand Rapids, MI: Eerdman's.
6. "Judaism 101," last modified 2011, http://www.jewfaq.org/qorbanot.htm. Copyright 5758-5771 1998-2011, Tracey R Rich.
7. Barnhouse, Donald Grey. 1965. *The Invisible War*. Grand Rapids, MI: Zondervan.
8. "Kübler-Ross Model," *Wikipedia,* last modified on May 5, 2014, http://en.wikipedia.org/wiki/K%C3%BCbler-Ross_model.
9. Fellman, Hazel and Allen, Edward Frank, eds. 1936. *Best Loved Poems of the American People*, 537. New York, NY: Doubleday.
10. Hughes, Selwyn. 2004. *Every Day With Jesus Bible*, 128. Nashville, TN: Holman Bible Publishers.
11. "Serenity Prayer," *Wikipedia,* last modified May 4, 2014, http://en.wikipedia.org/wiki/Serenity_Prayer.
12. Cowman, L.B. 1996. "March 30th entry." *Streams in the Desert*. Grand Rapids, MI: Zondervan.

Book References, Resources, & Recommendations

1. *Aquinas, For Armchair Theologians,* Timothy M. Renick
2. *The Dream Giver,* Bruce Wilkinson
3. *Every Day With Jesus, Walking in His Ways,* Selwyn Hughes
4. *The Four Things That Matter Most,* Ira Byock, M.D.
5. *The Gospel of John, Volume 2, Revised Edition,* William Barclay
6. *A Grace Disguised: How the Soul Grows through Loss,* Jerry L. Sittser
7. *The Great Divorce,* C.S. Lewis
8. *Hidden Treasures in the Book Of Job,* Hugh Ross
9. *How God Changes Your Brain: Breakthrough Findings from a Leading Neuroscientist,* Andrew Newberg, M.D. and Mark Robert Waldman
10. *The Interior Castle,* Teresa of Avila
11. *The Invisible War,* Donald Grey Barnhouse
12. *Jesus Calling,* Sarah Young
13. *The Jesus Prayer,* Frederica Mathewes-Green
14. *The Ladder of Divine Ascent,* John Climacus
15. *The Language of Letting Go,* Melody Beattie
16. *Living Beyond the Limits,* A Life in Sync With God Franklin Graham
17. *Man's Search for Meaning,* Viktor E. Frankl
18. *The Message Bible,* Eugene H. Peterson
19. *On Death and Dying,* Elisabeth Kübler Ross
20. *Pilgrims Regress,* C.S. Lewis
21. *Ryrie Study Bible,* Charles C. Ryrie
22. *A Scandalous Freedom: the Radical Nature of the Gospel,* Steve Brown
23. *Search for Significance,* Dr. Robert McGee
24. *Streams In The Desert,* Mrs. Charles E. Cowman
25. *Thru the Bible With J. Vernon McGee, Vol. 4,* J. Vernon McGee.

BONUS Sneak Peek of Cinthia's New Book, *Can Fairy Tales Be Real?*

Chapter One

We love stories—why? Stories inspire us, help us to think that maybe our life isn't so bad, or perhaps convince us that it could be better. Daniel Taylor wrote: "Our stories tell us who we are, why we are here, and what we are to do." As I reflected on my own life story, I realized I have had three stories going on in my life simultaneously, kind of like a braid. Let me explain. The 1st story is the reason why I'm here—the supernatural story that's bigger than me, the one that the Creator is unfolding in my life. The 2nd story is the story I'm writing with my choices in life. The 3rd story is my fairytale, and it's based in imagination, fantasy, and escapism.

So how did these three stories play out in my life?

They began with my hope of my fairytale story. You see, I was adopted. Although I had Christian parents that loved me and cared for me, there was always something missing. As a little girl I fantasized that I was secretly a princess that had been misplaced or lost. I dreamed that my real family was desperately looking for me; and when they found me, we would all live happily ever after. I always knew I was adopted, and even though my parents handled my adoption very well and always made me feel loved and wanted, it still affected me greatly as I grew up.

Being raised in a Christian home, I always heard how much God loved me. I would like to say that knowing this truth fixed things for me. But somehow my feelings of rejection, abandonment, not measuring up, and struggling to figure out "who I was" and "who I was supposed to be" became very problematic for me. I knew inside of me that I felt one way, that certain things came naturally to me, and that I was *very* different from my family.

This difference was revealed early on by the fact that both of my parents were brilliant, highly educated, and placed a great deal of importance on education. Though I was intelligent and considered gifted, all I ever wanted to do was sing, dance, act, or perform. Singing, gymnastics, swimming, and modern dance all felt so familiar, so perfect, so "me." All the while, my parents continuously asked me, "What about your education?" I didn't care; I just wanted to perform—I just wanted to *sing*. This was my fairytale, which I was going to *make* be "My Story." It was a very painful journey for my parents and me, *but God had a plan.*

I barely made it through high school with a "C" average, and college was no different. As I began dropping classes and joined a band, my parents were beside themselves. I finally got it together enough to pick a major: fashion merchandising. I thought my degree was creative enough to satisfy both my parents and me, and I could still work on my singing career along the way.

The last semester of my senior year, I felt God tap on my shoulder, telling me that He wanted my life. I was raised a Christian, and when I was little I had made that decision to follow Him and was baptized. However, as an adult, it was another story. I felt like I had a pretty good "gig" going; this was now "my story." I kept dreaming that it was my destiny to sing. *Now* God asks me for my life? I told Him that He would have to convince me. *Really.*

"My Story" continued on after graduation when I accepted a job as an assistant buyer for Robinsons–May in California, with 21 stores from Santa Barbara to San Diego, and drove a little white Porsche 924 with a sunroof! Life couldn't be better, right? Wrong. I was miserable. I was in a bad relationship, stressed out, and hated my job because it was all numbers and orders, nothing really creative at all. Even though I was successful and promoted, all I wanted to do was sing. I was depressed, anxious, overwhelmed, and empty, even though the outside looked great!

It was only then that I came to find out God's Story for me. You see, we rarely accept or look for God's Story unless "our story" and the "fairytale" are not working. Let me tell you, He convinced me—through trying and failing to do it on my own—that life without Him would be a nightmare. I mean, *really*—I thought I could do better than God? I finally offered my life to God, even though I had categorically messed it up.

"God, do you still want my life, the way it is—what I have done with it?"

I got a resounding, YES! You see, God wasn't waiting for me to "get it all together." He was actually waiting, patiently and kindly, for everything to fall apart. I came to learn that God wants me at my best *and* at my worst. His story for my life is a far better story than I could ever write for myself, or even fantasize about. In spite of all my bad choices and trying to make "my story" work, *God still wanted me.*

And He still wants you, too, even if your

story has been derailed by your own agenda.

Think about how the three stories are woven throughout your life. God is working through your story, His Story, and your fairytale. You see, God's story is our promise that He has a purpose for us filled with destiny. Our story is the participation within God's story for us. Our fairytales are intended to give us hope and vision. They give us the energy to continue to "walk out" the story God has for us—it's bigger than us, unique, not a copy or re-make; it is our unique piece of history with promise, continuing into eternity.

Visit http://cinthiahiett.com for updates about Cinthia's books, Cinthia's blog, her radio show, and information about how to book her for your next event!

Made in the USA
Charleston, SC
13 February 2017